Power Skills

This edition published in 2020 by OH!
An imprint of the Welbeck Publishing Group Limited
20 Mortimer Street
London W1T 3JW

British Library Cataloguing-in-Publication data available on request.

ISBN 978-1-85906-461-0

10 9 8 7 6 5 4 3 2 1

Printed in Europe

JULIET ERICKSON

Power Skills

A MASTERCLASS FOR WOMEN
IN BODY LANGUAGE AND COMMUNICATION

contents

3

Eye Contact

4

Voice and Facial Expression

5

Confrontation

6

Cultivating Presence

introduction

For the last 30 years I have worked with thousands of women from all walks of life: academics, students, entrepreneurs, leaders of non-profit organizations, scientists, politicians, entertainers and CEOs. My role as their coach has been to help them communicate the best version of themselves. They gained traction in high-stakes situations where succeeding or failing had a high professional or personal impact. The truth is, no matter how many billions of dollars are at stake, how great or important an idea, or even how famous or clever a person may be, their success largely boils down to whether they communicate persuasively with others.

Men have outnumbered women three to one among my clients, not because the men necessarily needed more help, but because more of them had the high-profile jobs, the access and the means required to hire a person like me. Interestingly, the women I have worked with have represented a more diverse group – a more integral blend of different races, identities, ethnicities, religions and nationalities and belonged to a broader range of socioeconomic groups.

I write this book because I feel passionately that now is 'prime-time' for women to step fully into their power. By prime-time, I mean that women have begun to overhaul the concept of what power means with a subtle but profound reordering of traditional definitions and structures. We wield power without a suit and tie or a high-profile job. We focus less on title and career, and more on responsibility to ourselves, our family, work, community and the world. We are both equal opportunity employers and self-employers.

By power, I mean a power without reference to gender, where we, as women, are embraced by ourselves and others as competent, effective and impactful. As women, our focus is more on self-mastery and self-esteem rather than title and status. As the feminist scholar Carolyn Heilbrun said, 'Power is the ability to take one's place in whatever discourse is essential to action and the right to have one's part matter.'

I believe our minds and spirits are in place but I observe that our bodies often defy us. We still struggle with our body language, communicating something different from what we intend or wish, particularly when we are stressed.

For all people, gender norms and behaviours are culturally formed and reinforced. It's no surprise to any person reading this book who gender-identifies as a woman that there are behavioural and attitudinal norms and assumptions that have a strong influence in shaping their lives. Some of these are inspiring, but many are debilitating.

At birth, most of our movements are instinctive; we experience hunger or fear and we respond by crying. As we grow, our movements gradually become more active, more intentional. As the mind develops, it begins to program the functioning of brain and body. In learning how to walk, talk, play and relate to other people and through repetition, we are gradually patterned to move reflexively and unconsciously. This process is the beginning of our conditioning, whether we like it or not. How we walk, talk, respond and behave is informed by the people who raised and influenced us.

As we continue to grow, even beyond childhood, we continue to be conditioned by our neuromuscular system and socialization. While these patterns that we develop may not always serve us, we function every day not really thinking about them and continue to reinforce them. Because these patterns are repeated and reinforced, it creates limitations and imbalances in our bodies.

Most of us are not very aware of the repetitive nature of our actions, both mental and physical. In this book, I will be encouraging you to take steps to develop your awareness in order to begin the process of breaking the cycles. Self-awareness is the key to any process of transformation.

This lifetime of shaping creates many of our body language habits. Whether the shaping serves us or not, we often remain unaware of it from day to day. With greater self-awareness, we can begin the journey of breaking the unconscious patterns of behaviour that don't serve us.

I want this book to be your go-to body language resource and toolbox that you can call on when you need it most. I hope you enjoy the illustrations as much as I do, as they reinforce important insights and learnings.

The first chapter on communication styles is about improving your powers of observation, both yourself and others, and, particularly, how your communication style informs your body language. By the end of the section, you will be able to readily identify your own communication strengths and vulnerabilities, as well as those of other people. You should also have a clearer idea about how to respond to other people in a way that will help you to achieve better outcomes.

Chapters 2, 3 and 4 contain a toolbox of techniques designed to increase your awareness of, and comfort with, your own body language. They will introduce you to 'foundational behaviours' that you can integrate into your movement, gestures, posture, eye contact, facial expressions and voice. A foundational behaviour is a physical action that provides a way to understand interplay between our conscious and unconscious choices. It will help you easily settle into a more natural, authentic physical self. As a result of choosing foundational behaviours, you will begin to feel differently in the moment and you will notice the responses you get from others will begin to change. By the end

of this section you'll be able to introduce subtle yet profound changes into your everyday body language.

The last two chapters about managing confrontation and cultivating presence are areas of practice that offer the greatest opportunity for women to transform themselves. It is in these two areas where I am most often asked for assistance. While both managing confrontation and cultivating presence require similar grit from you so that you become comfortable with them, they are different animals. Which would you rather tame, a tiger or a bull elephant? How about both? By the end of this section you will understand more about the nature of these two areas of transformation and be able to utilize techniques right away in a range of situations.

The insights offered in this book will make it easier for you to choose body language that creates the outward expression of confidence and, at the same time, the internal feeling of ease and calm. Over time and with practice, these behaviours will liberate you from the effects of your conditioning. They will help you to regain more control over, and comfort with, how you communicate through body language.

6 **What I have discovered is that if women can bring awareness to their physical presence and their bodies, it can dramatically shift and transform the effectiveness with which they communicate, persuade and influence others. 9**

Communication Styles

1

In this chapter, I'll explore communication styles and the role that awareness of your own communication style and that of others plays in your general sense of wellbeing and effectiveness.

Medicine, both ancient and modern, categorizes our body types and behaviour generally as a guide to the human condition, providing a framework for diagnosis and cure. Modern neurobiology is making great strides in understanding how the body, brain and nervous system are shaped and reshaped by our own intention and experience.

As women, we are certainly aware of the emotional and physical effort of having to overcome discrepancies in power and privilege in general. On top of that, built-in biases and expectations from others about how we should behave and a lifetime of socialization reinforcing our stereotypical modes of behaviour can make any change feel like a struggle. Have no fear – you already have inside you most of what you need to make changes.

I am frustrated by the popular advice given to women on the subject of body language, where there is a clear message: all that girly stuff you learned, stop it! Firm up your handshake, stop tilting your head, don't smile excessively, stop being girly and passive, speak up, learn to interrupt, take up more space, stop nodding, don't flirt, stop being so emotional. Can you think of anything else? I bet you can.

Okay, while some of that advice resonates, a lot of it is cliché based on other people's generalized views on how a woman should behave. The key here is that what is 'right or wrong' from a body language perspective depends on the context.

In business and professional settings, there are formal and informal, spoken and unspoken rules about interacting with others, what one can and cannot say, what is acceptable in terms of the clothes you wear. In social situations, with family, in a bar, on a dating app or at a party, there are yet another set of rules.

There are many wonderful things we have learned through our feminine conditioning, but I want you to become more consciously aware of those behaviours that may not be serving you and replace them with behaviours that will.

Think about communication style as a set of behaviours that are considered 'typical' of the way you behave. All of us have a fairly predictable set of behaviours, which are how you act most of the time without thinking about it. They might include things that people closest to you would say if they were asked to describe you. These typical behaviours come naturally to you and together shape how others perceive you and the impressions you create. They can also be an indication of the type of person with whom you get along, or don't; how you prefer to send and receive information; how you listen; how comfortable you feel with change or confrontation; the level of emotion you use in decision-making; your stress levels and attention span, among many other things.

These typical behaviours are your default mechanism – something that automatically happens unless you actively override it. We all have a predominant default type that will appear most often, particularly under pressure. This is important because this default can also determine what sort of habits you develop and reinforce unconsciously. Being more aware of these defaults will

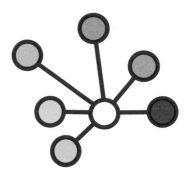

not only help you to become more aware of your own strengths and weaknesses, but also to devise your own strategies for replacing unwanted habits and moving on.

You can also use the insights in this chapter to build connections and create more ease with people whose default types are opposite to yours. If you are naturally easy-going and laid-back, you are going to get along with someone else whose communication style is similar. But we all have to work, live and play with people whose styles are not like ours. Instead of jarring with those whose style is very different, you can work with them, know what to expect from them and understand them and respond in ways that you know they will understand and connect with. There is no sacrifice of your natural self or manipulation involved. There's no 'faking-it'. Creating more ease means simply doing what comes naturally but doing it with awareness.

Building rapport

Communication styles provide an open window into one of the most important skills you will develop in your lifetime, and that is your ability to build rapport with others. Rapport is defined as a close and harmonious relationship in which people communicate well. However, in most situations, especially when we need something from someone else or we are feeling stressed, rapport doesn't come about so smoothly and easily. Choosing to build rapport means choosing to create the best possible outcome for any meeting or situation you are in. So, rapport is part conscious, part unconscious. Let's look at how it happens.

Mirroring This is something we all do daily with friends and family without being aware of it. By being consciously aware of mirroring, you can use it to build connections with the people you want to influence. Mirroring is all about body language, those verbal and non-verbal signals we send when we are with another person. How do you adjust your posture, gesture, voice tone, eye contact when they are feeling happy, angry or sad? Have you ever been deep in conversation with someone only to notice that you are both holding the same pose, leaning forwards on one elbow, head resting in your hand? Look around a restaurant at couples talking to one another or groups of friends walking and laughing together and notice the subtle and sometimes not-so-subtle mirroring of their physical and emotional states.

We humans are natural imitators. We yawn when others yawn, we smile when someone smiles at us. Throughout our lives we tend to take on the energy, focus, gesture and posture of people to whom we feel close or are at ease or intimate with. Neurologists call this ability to imitate 'mirroring' – an action involving a complex set of brain activities that come together to help us experience and interpret behaviours, actions and emotions. In a recent study, researchers used brain-imaging technology to study listeners and speakers. They found that the brain adapts to signals from another person and uses body language to enhance understanding – like a brain-to-brain coupling. Unconscious mirroring is ideal. Doing it with conscious awareness requires some skills. Mirroring is not mimicking or mocking. If you are not really

How to mirror

Build a connection first by making listening and understanding your first priority. Then you can start nodding and tilting your head as you listen. Match their tone of voice, pace or energy level. Then, if things are moving along well, try mirroring some of their postures or gestures. Stay genuine and don't rush. A good rule of thumb is not to mirror their negative body language. Most important: trust that you'll figure it out!

interested or engaged, trying to mirror another person can backfire. The other person is likely to notice it and see it as an attempt at manipulation. If you are not sure, take it slow. I like to think, 'Meet them where they are'.

You will learn that you can use behaviours to build a bridge and connect to someone who is not like you by subtly behaving more like they do. It is not something you do to someone but something you do with someone.

Empathy Another aspect of developing rapport is feeling empathy. Empathy is your ability to understand how the other person feels, rather than how you feel in a particular situation. We are reminded throughout our lives to try to imagine what it is like to walk in another's shoes. The challenge is to be willing and open to knowing and understanding others. Research indicates that our ability to build empathy with others has a learned bias built in. In other words, we are likely to experience the feelings of another with whom we see as similar. Good news, our preference for sameness is taught and we can change our perceptions!

Four Communication Styles

There are four communication styles that I use to help my clients and students and which will help you to understand your own body language and that of others. As you read through the descriptions, you may notice yourself and most of the people you know.

1

Direct

results-driven, commanding, challenging, opposing, confrontational, wilful, self-confident

Recognizing a direct style

- May come across as impatient and may even interrupt you or cut meetings or conversations short

- Likely to be tidy and organized

- Uses little or no small talk

- Questions and answers are short and to the point

- Prefers people to be specific when explaining something

- Prefers recommendations and main points to be 'up front' during meetings/conversations

- Doesn't mind an argument or confrontation

- Is usually forceful or energetic

- May appear calm in tense situations

- Tends to use full eye contact comfortably

- Likes to control agendas and conversations and responds well to order and punctuality

- Is well structured in thinking and verbal expression

- Often stands with weight on both feet equally

- Has squared shoulders and hips, directly facing others while speaking or listening
- Vocal variation is often based on louder volume
- Makes more statements than asks questions and tends to ask questions that elicit one-word answers or use lines of questioning that can feel like an interrogation.

How to connect with a direct style

- Stand erect, shoulders relaxed, weight on both feet evenly, face the person directly
- Be prepared to be forceful and energetic, if needed
- Ensure your voice is clear and audible
- Be on time for meetings or social engagements
- Don't think out loud (ramble)
- Minimize small talk and avoid being too familiar
- Make your letters and emails short and to the point
- Answer their questions briefly and specifically, ensuring you understand the question first
- In conversation, make your point first and then explain the detail (if they want it)
- Check your understanding upfront about the time available for a meeting
- Be up on current events and use real examples in your stories to punctuate with relevance
- If you don't know something, say so
- Send short, succinct follow-up emails or notes.

2
Expressive
self-promoting,
persuasive, inspiring,
ambitious, charming,
optimistic, talkative

Recognizing an expressive style

- Works in a slightly disorganized environment

- Likes personal and positive small talk

- Tends to breathe shallowly

- Excitable, articulate, animated and tends to speak quickly

- Enjoys creative challenges

- Dislikes detail

- Can be judgemental

- Enjoys hearing about personal achievements

- Can be competitive

- Enjoys big-picture thinking and exploring new ideas

- Pride and ego can be very important

- Easily distracted

- May frequently gesture

- Has an expressive face and body, often 'overdoing' gestures and movement

- Enjoys spontaneity and looking at things differently

- Often stands with weight on one foot or the other and can be off-balance

- Leans and sits on furniture, touches and fiddles with objects

- Vocal variation comes quite easily

- Asks questions easily and spontaneously, rather than deliberately, but often comes unstuck with

multiple questions or follow-up open or
closed questions

- Confrontation can get personal
- Masks responses more easily than other
  communication styles.

How to connect with an expressive style

- Be creative, colourful and explore ideas
- Keep details to a minimum
- Be prepared to appear confident and/or dynamic
- Avoid competing with them (at least early on)
- In meetings or conversations, be prepared to
  discuss the big picture at the start and then spend
  the rest of the meeting bringing it to life
- Be open to meeting in 'third spaces' (somewhere
  other than the office)
- Show you recognize their contribution to a
  success story
- Send thank-you notes (maybe with something
  creative based on your conversation or outcome).

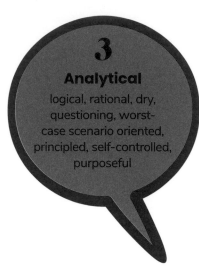

3

Analytical

logical, rational, dry,
questioning, worst-
case scenario oriented,
principled, self-controlled,
purposeful

Recognizing an analytical style

- Often has a tidy and organized office and home

- Is logic-, fact- and order-orientated – background and rationale first, recommendation second

- Often asks for detail and support material

- Enjoys technical challenges

- Asks questions and gives answers that are precise and sometimes unimaginative

- Is physically low-key

- Rarely uses words such as intuitive, believe, think, feel, etc.

- Uses words like rationale, know, prove, demonstrate, analyze

- Takes extra time in meetings/projects to ensure thorough understanding/analysis is done

- Minimal physical activity while speaking or listening, particularly gesture and movement and facial expression

- Has strong eye contact while listening – but often not while speaking

- Tends towards a softer voice

- Doesn't like to rush

- Asks deliberate questions

- Doesn't like confrontation and may put off difficult conversations.

How to connect with an analytical style

- Be on time for meetings and social engagements
- Make sure you have facts and other types of support to back up what you are saying during discussions
- Avoid words like intuitive, gut feeling, feel, believe, wish
- Use words like know, prove, intend, demonstrate, analyze
- Don't exaggerate or use sweeping statements
- Don't answer questions too quickly or interrupt
- Take your time and try not to rush the pace of the interaction
- Keep a low-key style, without too much enthusiasm or perkiness
- Send any follow-up email or message with acknowledgement of any key agreements and unanswered questions or follow-up.

4
Social/Amiable
helpful, mentoring, compliant, sympathetic, warmth, yearning, self-reflecting, non-threatening, conciliatory, calm

Recognizing a social/amiable style

- The environment is relaxed, with everyone's comforts attended to

- Warm, friendly and talkative, patient and unrushed

- May take some time to get 'down to business'

- Other people's thoughts and feelings inform their decision-making

- Harmony is important

- Interested in your personal experience on matters

- Proud of relationships and friends

- Doesn't like confrontation and may put off difficult conversations

- Has good eye contact while personal in nature, but this reduces during conflict or discomfort

- Desires consensus and harmony, which can lead to delays or procrastination

- Fair and quick to defend others

- Facial expression, gesture and movement are focused on building empathy and rapport with others

- Is a loyal supporter and skilled empathizer

- Doesn't always speak up for themselves

- Is comfortable talking about opinions, feelings and concerns.

How to connect with a social/amiable style

- If you are late for a meeting, have a good personal reason

- Be warm, friendly and willing to talk

- Ask about their family and personal interests

- Show you are interested in how others feel

- Get together for reasons other than business

- Send thank-you notes (with a personal touch based on what you have learned about them)

- Try not to be too direct, too soon

- Involve others who may be affected by decisions or actions in the process

- Recognize their contributions in meetings

- Share information about yourself.

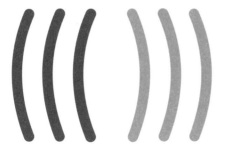

Companion styles

It's important to keep in mind that you are not just one style all the time. As I mentioned, we often default to the tendencies of one style more than the others, particularly when under pressure or feeling tense. For each style, there is a companion style, where you will notice other familiar characteristics of yourself.

It is extremely rare to have the characteristics of the style diagonally opposite your style as shown on the graph opposite, and these opposite styles have the most difficulty building an easy relationship with each other, but that means there is real opportunity here!

So, there are some specific characteristics that identify communication styles, and you can see that we all have built-in preferences and default behaviours. But remember, these aren't bad or good, right or wrong, they just are.

Knowing your own style is a good step towards helping you understand yourself and your ingrained physical patterns. This increased self-awareness is a positive step towards identifying behaviours that don't serve you and replacing them with behaviours and responses that do.

You will also be able to observe others more objectively and skilfully, allowing you to adapt your style more consciously when you want to build an understanding or affinity with someone. Imagine the power of that and get to it!

PEOPLE-ORIENTED

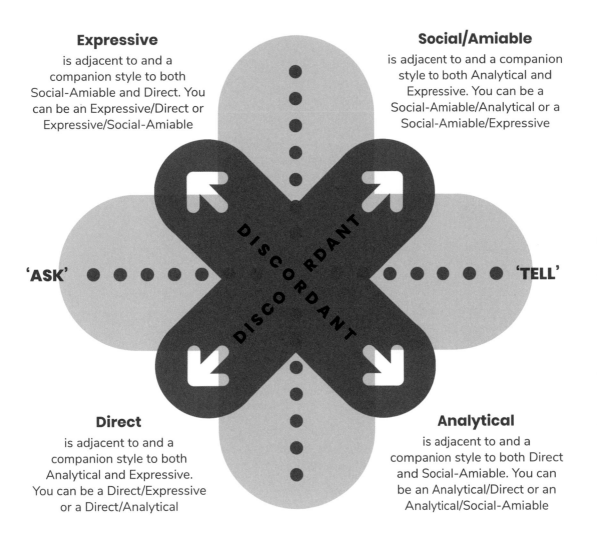

Expressive

is adjacent to and a companion style to both Social-Amiable and Direct. You can be an Expressive/Direct or Expressive/Social-Amiable

Social/Amiable

is adjacent to and a companion style to both Analytical and Expressive. You can be a Social-Amiable/Analytical or a Social-Amiable/Expressive

'ASK'

DISCORDANT
DISCORDANT

'TELL'

Direct

is adjacent to and a companion style to both Analytical and Expressive. You can be a Direct/Expressive or a Direct/Analytical

Analytical

is adjacent to and a companion style to both Direct and Social-Amiable. You can be an Analytical/Direct or an Analytical/Social-Amiable

TASK-ORIENTED

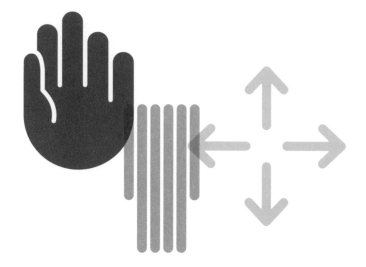

2

Posture, Gesture and Movement

This chapter is intended to help you bring awareness to how you use posture, gesture and movement independently, and in doing so, strengthen your ability to gather them together in the moment to work for you.

Our bodies are sculptural representations of how we feel and think, or, as the saying goes, 'Your body can't go where the mind isn't.' How we carry ourselves and the habits we hold are formed over many years, often from a lack of awareness about our bodies, a lack of exercise or the wrong exercise, bad chairs, poor diet or health, lack of self-confidence or perhaps just too much travel or tiredness. Medication and recreational drugs are also becoming a defining factor for some.

I like to refer to posture, movement and gesture as the 'Three Sisters' of body language. There are Three Sisters stories across many cultures, each one slightly different, but they are always about women who endure some kind of hardship and separation from each other before they join up together again at the end, stronger than they were before.

My favourite is from the Native American Iroquois creation myth that three plants – corn, squash and beans – when planted together thrive in the same way that three sisters can be found to be inseparable. The gardening term is companion planting, the cultivation of different types of plants nearby to benefit each other.

In my experience, posture, movement and gesture often operate like companion plants. For example, the key to improving a person's posture can sometimes be supported by a shift in their body movement or in the way they gesture or hold their arms, hands or head. Awareness brought to one of these Three Sisters can often lead to a benefit in another. The extent of it varies from person to person but the link is undeniable. It is rare that these three sisters can be separated for long.

Posture

I grew up in California during the end of an era of an organized good-posture movement in the US. It was run by a group called The American Posture League and taken up by medical and educational professionals throughout the country. At school and at home, adults were constantly reminding children to sit up straight and walk tall. The dark side of this movement was that kids were publicly ostracized for bad posture and rewarded for good posture. Certain kids were given the role of 'posture cops', a peer-monitoring activity, and asked to tag classmates who had good posture and those who didn't. The message to me as a young girl was that good posture meant being popular and accepted. Slouching became something to avoid.

According to friends of mine who also grew up during this period the misinformed coaching we received to create our too-erect and upright posture in our childhood is catching up with us in the form of stiff necks and backs.

Power and posture

Fast-forward to one of the most exciting developments this decade: research in the area of postural feedback, which suggests that a powerful posture sparks a biochemical reaction in your body that actually makes you more powerful. What happens is when we adopt certain postures, it triggers a more powerful biological you by increasing certain hormones and reducing others. In that moment, and for a while thereafter, you can 'feel' more confident and less stressed. The opposite also applies to less powerful postures that can bring your energy down and reinforce a feeling of lack of confidence.

The body will kick-start the confidence and self-esteem process for you and support you when you need it. Of course, your body language needs cooperation from your emotional state. With increased awareness, you can begin to calibrate your physical and emotional states step by step. Take the posture, savour it, notice how it feels and how it may affect your perspective in the moment. Repeat as needed.

Simply put, a woman with a straight back is seen to be healthy, confident, attractive and strong, while a woman who is slouching is viewed as unhealthy, powerless and unattractive. As women, we often resign ourselves to the idea that if we don't feel or look powerful, we can't act that way. However, these findings imply that by changing how you use your body, you can change your psychology and, ultimately, the circumstances of your life.

Good and bad posture

There is not a lot of disagreement about what constitutes good posture, and there is a breadth of science about optimal postural health for our bones, joints and muscles. I was happy to learn there is even a World Posture Day on 23 March each year. However, despite what appears to be a lot of common sense and publicly available insight about how to have good posture, we still experience postural problems. These are often created by imbalances in our body that spring from doing too much of something badly for too long, structural problems or inflexible muscles. Add to that

' It is easier to act yourself into a new way of thinking than to think yourself into a new way of acting. ' Maya Angelou

the physical and emotional changes that life throws at us, the forces of self-image and self-esteem, it is a wonder sometimes that we can stand up at all.

Good posture is not posing. It's important to be aware of how good posture relies on a solid framework of support (our aligned skeleton), just like any other physical structure in this world that is governed by the same natural laws of physics.

Most common posture challenges experienced by women involve subtle misalignments of the body, usually into what can be interpreted as low-energy, low-power postures. My tall friend Emmy spent many of her early years hunching her shoulders and folding her neck forwards. This was an attempt to make herself appear smaller because she was told it would help her dating prospects. Another friend's breasts developed much earlier than her peers, so she spent years rounding her shoulders to hide them. Nita grew up in a family who told her it wasn't ladylike to draw attention to herself, so she made herself less intrusive by rounding her shoulders and folding her arms low and tight in front of her body.

Whatever the reason or conditioning, these misalignments can cause muscular and joint problems over time if they are not rebalanced. Our emotional state is a consideration, too. For example, slouching is considered a diagnostic factor of clinical depression. On the upside, sitting and standing upright increases positivity in your mood.

Default behaviours

Have you ever noticed how comedians and entertainers can mimic so skilfully by focusing on only one or two recognizable physical traits? As soon as they start, everyone knows exactly whom they are imitating. We all have a particular posture or set of postures, usually about three or four obvious ones, that represent our habits and personal comfort zone. Think about it as the way you stand or sit most often. Another way to think about it is what a friend would do if asked to imitate you physically.

The challenge is that we are so unaware of our default postures. Keep in mind that there is nothing good or bad, right or wrong about them, but they usually form the bulk of our unconscious postures, and regardless of whether they serve us or not, we keep repeating them.

Standing defaults

The most common default postures for women include exaggerated weight transfers from one hip to another while standing (or sitting); standing with your weight back on your heels or forwards on your toes; rounded shoulders and a concave chest, or ribs forced outwards, creating an exaggerated expansive chest; head tilted at an angle; shoulders angled to one side, causing us to glance sideways often. Recognize anything yet?

We go into these defaults often without thinking about them, when we are listening to someone or something (using our devices, standing or seated in a meeting or conversation) and when we are delivering a presentation or just talking to someone, particularly when communicating an idea, thought or answering a question. In other words, these postures appear often when we are intentionally sending or receiving communication.

Let's start with stillness. You will make more progress breaking and refining habits that don't serve you if you can begin by understanding the importance of creating balance, calm, poise when your body is still. Our body at rest can be a battlefield of mixed unconscious messages, making it harder for us to listen and observe and, ultimately, to close the gap between what we intend to communicate and what we actually communicate. Here are some of the most common postural defaults for women:

Locked at the ankles This is where the ankles are crossed tightly, bringing one foot over the other when standing. As a result of this position, the chest raises and one shoulder is slightly elevated. The net effect on the body is to make it off balance. I have been told by some clients that this posture is easy to maintain, especially while wearing heels. However, aside from being physically damaging, this resting posture can create the impression of not wishing to readily engage or not believing that there is any expectation to engage. It also implies uncertainty, perhaps unworthiness.

The standing slouch This posture has hunched, rounded shoulders, neck and head forwards, hands low in front of you or at your sides. It is also often referred to as 'computer back' or 'text-neck'. This posture creates the impression of low energy, low power and low confidence. Standing like this makes it difficult to communicate emphasis or priority because there is very little movement and the hands are low and tight around the body. It is also one that many women default to in order to consciously or unconsciously avoid imposing on others or to keep from taking up too much space.

Containing and reducing oneself can be interpreted as a generous and humble gesture. However, women have over the centuries been the keepers of the physical postures of gentleness, kindness and submission. In a modern world, I would rather that women use these postures as and when they choose.

Working the S-curve This refers to exaggerating the 'S' of our spines in order to jut out our breasts and buttocks, which is supposed to result in a supercharged feminine appeal. There are variations of the S-curve, from subtle to exaggerated. I'm not sure about you, but I can't hold even a mildly exaggerated version of this posture with a serious face for very long. One of the funniest videos I have ever seen was of women being photographed trying to replicate and hold the exaggerated S-curve poses of female comic book and video game characters.

The S-curve is infinitely recognizable as 'feminine'. However, maintaining this posture is unhealthy for

our backs and puts our bodies off balance. In some contexts, holding it for very long could prove to be an unfortunate distraction for ourselves and others. Working the S-curve can set off a chain reaction of other conscious and unconscious movements, depending on how you want to use it.

The foundational standing posture

This neutral posture creates in the body a feeling of strength and being earthed. It allows you to be more flexible, so that you move forwards, backwards or sideways with greater ease. Consider this your go-to posture for clearing your mind, regaining your emotional and physical balance, sharpening your awareness and calming your body.

Our goal for the foundational posture (and all the body language and postures we will discuss) is for it to be a place where you can cultivate physical and emotional clarity and increased confidence when you need it. You will circumnavigate postures that bring the perception of 'attitude' and attention to a situation and actually help you to avoid these mindsets.

Your skeletal, nervous, digestive and respiratory systems are more easily regulated in a neutral posture. You can improve your ability to pay attention and create more ease between yourself and others by removing distractions. You will communicate attentiveness, energy and interest in the moment. Others will find you non-threatening. They will engage with you more quickly.

Try the exercise overleaf for promoting a neutral posture on an even surface.

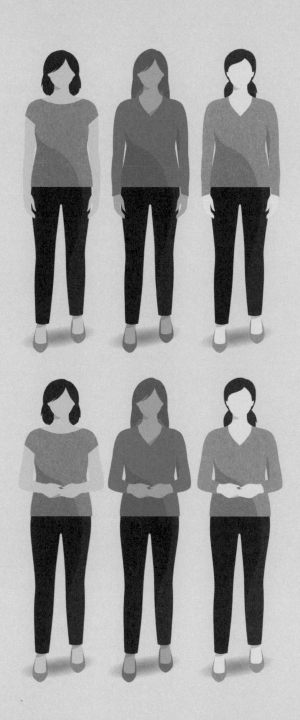

1   Stand with both feet on the floor, with your weight distributed evenly between both feet, hip-width apart. (Be aware of not falling into the 'S' curve by noting any desire to exaggerate side or forward angles in the torso.)

2   Relax your shoulders and let your arms drop. You may feel some delicious length in your neck and spine and some gentle length between your hip and ribcage.

3   Allow the pelvis to relax into a neutral place, not tilted too far forwards or back.

4   Notice how you feel when the weight is distributed on your whole foot. Pause here for a moment to experience this wonderful feeling of balance and stability.

5   Take your dominant foot and step it just in front of the other – about where the heel of your dominant foot lines up with the big toe of your other foot – keeping them hip-width apart. Don't lock your knees.

6   Concentrate on keeping the weight mostly on both feet. You should be able to move your body gently forwards and back without losing balance.

7   Now shift your weight ever so slightly to the middle of the front foot without affecting the position of the back foot too much – perhaps your back heel is still on the floor but has less weight on it than the front foot. Feel how your upper body rises a little with this subtle

weight shift forwards, how your body lengthens and your shoulders are free to relax, and the ribcage, chest and chin are naturally positioned without stress on the body.

8   Have your arms and hands relaxed at your sides, with the wrists relaxed. An option is to bend the elbows in a 90-degree angle – keeping the shoulders relaxed – and bring the hands together gently in the front. This 90-degree angle for one or both hands is still a resting posture, yet it keeps the hands free and ready. It communicates a little more energy, stability and attention.

Posture health

- Strengthen your core abdominal and back muscles. Core strength training, Pilates and yoga-based exercises all help to maintain a healthy spine.

- Keep moving. Walk, take the stairs, choose to activate your body if you have the choice between moving or not moving.

- Create a healthy workspace. Build an environment that supports good posture.

- Focus on your feet. Invest in quality shoes that feel comfortable.

- Keep your knees from locking. While standing, keep a gentle bend in your knees.

- Mix it up. If you sit for more than 30 minutes, get up, stretch, move.

- Pay attention and stop yourself slouching, slumping, jutting your head forwards.

Sitting defaults

Some of your most important communication is done sitting down socially with friends or family. At work, more and more of our meetings, interviews, conference calls and presentations are being conducted seated as well. The following are some of the most common seated postural defaults for women.

Far forwards This involves leaning heavily forwards on the elbows with the torso folded over the body at an angle. With a table in front of the body, this means leaning at an angle that is often too far in. Without a table, the body is leaning

forwards and resting on the knees. The impression this can create is that you may be 'checked-out', distracted, sleepy or even intense. This closed position also limits your ability to modulate your voice.

Tight-upright This means being too close to the table. One of my clients was a very petite woman who used to pull herself very close (belly touching) to the table during meetings. She also used to stack her papers, devices, notepad and extra pens in ordered stacks around her, creating neat little piles that extended out to her arm's length. Because she sat so close to the table it limited her ability to see people, or others to see her down the table on her immediate right or left. She wasn't comfortable making those readjustments, which meant leaning far forwards or pushing away from the table. Unfortunately, she stayed firmly planted in what I call a 'blind spot'.

Far back This means sitting too far back from the table or in the chair so that you give the impression of being disengaged. This extreme can also include being low in the chair, crossing the legs and sitting heavily on one hip, arms folded across the body.

The challenge with being in any of the above extreme seated positions is that any change or shift you make in your body appears exaggerated. For example, if you are seated too far back to be noticed, you have to lean far forwards to speak or adjust yourself so you can be seen. Also, because the positions are exaggerated (forward, tight-upright, back), they aren't usually comfortable for your body to be in for too long.

Shrinking This means shoulders slouched with your hands in your lap. This has the postural triple whammy of collapsing your solar plexus, pulling your shoulders down and putting strain on your spine. This creates the impression of not wanting to be wherever you are or not feeling worthy of being there.

Perky This creates the impression of a little too much eagerness. Hips are usually all the way to the back of the chair, spine erect, shoulders upright, back slightly arched, hands folded/clasped on top of the table or in lap.

The foundational seated posture

Consider this your go-to seated posture for clearing the mind, regaining your emotional and physical balance, sharpening your awareness and calming your body. It is important that you take your chair choice seriously. If you are in a meeting, make sure your chair is comfortable and adjustable, that it is the right height for you and won't get tangled up in whatever you are wearing.

Try this while seated at a desk or conference table:

1   Distribute your weight evenly on both hips.

2   Move your body so that the edge of the seat is placed about midway up your hamstrings. Your spine may not be touching the back of the chair – that's okay.

3   Your feet can be flat on the floor next to each other or one foot slightly forward of the other – whichever is more comfortable.

4   Be close enough to the table so you can rest your mid-forearm lightly and comfortably on it.

5   Fold your hands gently over one another or next to each other on the table. Relax your fingers.

6   Relax your shoulders and neck, and keep your chin level.

If there is no table, sit as far back on the chair as you need to for support but keep your spine

active (not slouched), resting your arms in your lap without folding or clenching your hands. Keep your chin level. Cross your legs if you wish but make sure you don't shift weight all the way over onto one hip.

If you are seated on soft furnishings, (an upholstered couch, sofa or chair that also doesn't have a lot of firm structure) be sure to choose something that supports your back and legs comfortably. Bear in mind that certain soft furnishings are hard to get out of without sometimes awkward effort or wardrobe malfunction!

Posture tips for wheelchair users

Many of the same rules apply to anyone sitting for long periods in a wheelchair or any chair. Correct posture requires that each part of your body is in the right position, from head to toe.

- Make sure your pelvis is supported and your weight can be spread evenly in your thighs and buttocks.

- Sit upright, draw your shoulders back and be sure you are not slumping or leaning to one side. If you can't maintain this position, be sure the back of your wheelchair has the right amount of postural support for your whole spine.

- Be sure the height and position of the footplates are sufficient so your hips and knees are at right angles and your weight is evenly distributed. Make sure your armrests are the correct height to support your arms, keep your shoulders level and neck natural and relaxed.

- Your head should be upright, in the middle, chin level or slightly tucked, with enough stability to look in different directions. If your head tilts forwards or backwards this can cause discomfort in the spine.

Gesture

Our hands are our body's punctuation and exclamation marks. They add emphasis and flavour to what we are saying and can help clarify or distract from our words. 'What do I do with my hands?' is a question I get asked so regularly that I have put it on a graphic t-shirt. It is also a question I take seriously because our hands are a wonderful source of energy, strength and vulnerability in our communication. Gesture is also a form of rich tradition across cultures, so be mindful that gestures don't always mean the same thing everywhere in the world.

Resting hands

One of the most important points to keep in mind about gesturing is knowing how and when to rest your hands. Once you get the hang of resting with ease, everything else will fall into place. This means being comfortable with your hands when they are not doing anything. What will happen when you master resting your gestures is that their purpose as clarifiers, emphasizers and illustrators, and when it is natural to use them, will become easier to distinguish. Resting is a form of gesture – think of it that way.

For example, if you gesture a lot when you communicate and resting feels like an uncomfortable idea to you right now, start small. On the other hand (no pun intended), if you don't gesture very much and the idea of doing more feels uncomfortable, start small. In both cases, for practise in your next conversation, presentation or meeting, be deliberate about which points or words would benefit from an accompanying gesture. At the same time, think about where resting your hands would benefit your message. Perhaps practise resting at the beginning, while asking a question or as you wind up the discussion. Putting your attention into marrying your words and gestures will add meaning and interest to what you are saying.

Over the years, I have enjoyed attending live poetry readings, not just for the poetry but because body language is an important part of the poet-listener experience. The interplay between the words and the interpretation, pacing, vocal tone, gesture and facial expression all bring the words to life and yet are not supposed to overshadow the language. I love this because, as a student of body language, I see the performer deliver a delicate balance of body language that reveals only what it needs to be revealed, with the goal of adding impact to the words, and no more.

A gesture exercise I have done with my clients over the years is to have them 'read' a poem silently, without moving their lips and only using gesture (and facial expression) to convey the rhythm, pace and feeling of the poem. Try it sometime and watch how interesting it is to attempt to bring words to life, without words. Consider making a video recording so you can view how it all works out.

Gesturing defaults

Our hands are used to having a job to do. The gesture defaults reveal themselves when we're not sure what to do with our hands in a particular situation. We may be unaware of what our hands are doing as we talk or even as we quietly listen to someone. Default gestures act as a kind of energy leak in our communication. They can distract both you and your listener. The following are some of the most common default gestures:

Gesturing out loud This is using gestures that are incongruous with what is being said. Often this type of gesturing is consistent with 'thinking out loud' or working through your thoughts. The hands and arms move as if searching through thoughts for a word, often in a circular or jagged motion. The danger here is that if there is a point or emphasis needed, the gestures don't reflect that. The point is often lost in the mind of both the speaker and listener. This kind of gesturing stokes the mind to wandering and is often associated with making the speaker go over time in meetings and presentations.

Tiny and out of sight This involves clenching the hands and fingers together, 'steepling' (hands lightly touching, fingers touching only at the tips) or clasping intertwined fingers, usually below the waist, in front or behind the body. It is interpreted as low-energy and can also indicate reluctance or shyness.

What often happens when the hands are clasped together behind the back is that they don't appear in front very often to gesture, or when they do, one hand has grasped the opposite elbow and only half an arm does the gesturing. Clenching your hands together can also act as a trigger to your nervous system to stay tense. There are differing opinions about steepling the fingers. Some feel it communicates incisiveness and confidence. The biggest challenge with steepling, though, is that it tends to become the dominant gesture of the user. As a result, they don't do much else with their hands.

Fidgeting Hair, jewellery, pens, devices, earlobes, buttons and other graspable objects become fair game for unconscious nervous tension. The challenge with fidgeting is that it can appear often enough in any conversation to become a distraction. Often, we don't realize we are doing it.

Foundational gestures

Resting your hands with ease is a foundational gesture. If you are standing, I refer you to the foundational posture on pages 34–37. Notice where the hands are placed – at about navel height, folded gently together with your fingers relaxed.

Another option is to hold your hands with the space between the thumb and the base of the index finger touching lightly. While seated, the hands can be gently folded near each other on your lap or on the table. This way they are easily accessible, visible and ready to gesture when needed. When your hands are held this way, you will feel more at ease. Always keep in mind that calm and relaxed hands come from calm and relaxed shoulders and neck.

Resting can include just leaving your hands at your sides, resting them on the back of a nearby chair or lightly on the top of a table, folded gently in front of you or behind your back. Even buried in a pocket of your jacket or trousers is okay in the right context. It is also comforting to hold a notebook or a pad of paper if you feel your hands are shaking before a meeting or presentation. Holding this relatively sturdy weight gives your muscles something to do.

Gestures are best used when the listener can see your face and eyes along with the gestures. The best gesture-zone is the central area of the body, above your waist, below the face and into an area just outward from your body, when needed. When you have finished gesturing, bring your hands back to rest. Make sure the gesture is started and finished completely and is consistent with what you are saying.

When you use your hands, be definite about it. Being definite means not gesturing all the time, but when you do, making sure it adds something to your message and that you mean it. People pay attention when you gesture and it makes what you are saying more memorable. If you want to improve the effectiveness of your gestures but aren't sure where to start, here are my some of my favourite methods.

Listing This can serve as a nonverbal 'anchor', or 'hook'. Use one hand to make the list or gently place one finger on another as you count, but don't press too hard on the opposite finger so as to bend it backwards.

Pointing If you need to direct attention somewhere or gesture to include someone, do so with an open palm and closed fingers. If you are pointing at a visual aid, turn your palm towards it (not palm outwards) and use two fingers to draw the listener's eye to what you want them to look at. If you are in front of a large group or you are public speaking, close your hand and use your thumb to 'aim' at the audience, rather than point.

This and that This gesture will help your listener keep track when you are talking about different ideas. For example, I may want to refer to results before and after an event and use one hand to express what happened before and my other hand to refer to after.

Increase or decrease Gesture to show, hands move away or towards each other during your description of something to show big or small, increase or decrease.

Gesture towards your heart If the subject matter is emotional, cover or touch your heart area with your hands to express that it is important to you.

Try to incorporate deliberate gestures in conversations to start getting used to gesturing with a purpose. You'll add a memorable and element to your communication.

Movement

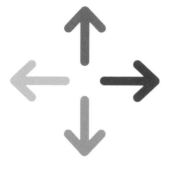

Without a doubt, movement is medicine for our mind, body and spirit. For those of us blessed with mobility, being able to choose consciously how we move our body can prove to be one of our most powerful communication tools.

Movement has an extra bonus besides being completely natural to us. Using movement in a meaningful way enhances your communication by adding another dimension to it. Meaningful movement turbocharges your message and creates a strong feeling in yourself and others.

Movement is where our social conditioning as women clashes with our natural strengths and inclinations. Research shows women naturally use a broader and less predictable range of spaces than men, but social conditioning stresses that we don't take up too much space or impose ourselves on others.

Women's relative natural ease with movement is consistent with my experience while coaching women. Women use movement and space to embody confidence and focus while they communicate. They are quick learners and generally easier to coach (than men) about using movement to set tone and mood in their communication. Women generally begin with less personal comfort about using movement, but often quickly excel at using a full range of techniques.

In stressful situations, if we can't move when we want or need to, tension 'leaks' out of us through our body movements in the form of pacing, twitching, incongruous movements, walking and talking too fast, shallow breathing and other signs of nervous energy. When you are feeling confident and relaxed, your movements are naturally more deliberate and focused.

Think about movement as how you move your body through your environment: how you navigate the distance between yourself and others; how you move from one place to another; how and where you stop; your gait and how you hold your body as you move. Maybe you have heard the phrases, 'She really owned the room', or 'We were hanging onto her every word', or 'She looks really relaxed and confident up there'. If you looked closely, you would see how the way she moved her body influenced how she was perceived.

The answer to what makes movement powerful is, 'It depends.' For example, if you are in a situation that calls for you to persuade individuals whose communication style (see Chapter 2) is very different from your own, you may be required to adapt an element of your movement to match theirs. So, if you are more analytical or physically low-key and need to build rapport and collaborate with a group of expressive, higher-energy people, you might consider ways you could physically 'meet them where they are', starting by using, say, 20 per cent plus higher-energy movements and gestures.

The same guidelines apply when you are out with friends at a restaurant or in another social situation that calls for a more intimate gathering. Your participation in, and the nature of, the conversation, your distance from the person next to or across from you all affect your choice of movement and gesture.

Movement defaults

Movement defaults stem from discomfort about how to use the space fully around you and position yourself in relation to people and objects. The context dictates some of the guidelines for movement.

If you are in a public-speaking situation, your movements need to consider the distance between you and your audience, the size of the room and how well people can see you. A small movement or gesture will have little or no effect if people can't see you clearly. So, there is opportunity for your movement (and gesture) to be a little more exaggerated.

Sometimes you may want to use movement for effect in a smaller space, such as a meeting or presentation room. In such situations, we commonly get glued to one spot, usually the front of the room, are often seated and using a projected visual aid or handout of some kind. The thought of adding movement here feels odd. Consider if you can see yourself in any of these most common movement defaults:

Walking while talking By this I don't mean chatting with someone while on a hike or a walk together but the kind of walking while talking when your attention needs to be on your listeners, such as during a presentation, meeting or conversation. It means that it appears you are thinking as you go along. The key is to know when and how you are using it for effect. What often happens, though, as you move about is that your important messages get lost and what you mean to say is delivered to the floor or the wall – anywhere but to your listener.

Neither here nor there This means positioning oneself at a 'neither here nor there' distance from others or from the main point of focus in the room. Many women tend not to get close enough to where the action is (or to be heard) and stop just short of it. Stopping short means not completing an action or leaving 'distance' between themselves and full engagement. This gives an impression of being tentative, not willing to engage or 'waiting' for an invitation to engage. This habit appears in many aspects of body language as a lack of definiteness or confident about completing a physical expression.

Swaying or side-stepping This is a kind of movement you have without really moving. Well, you are moving but more like a metronome. With this default, the feet are usually planted on the floor, while the body gently sways back and forth. This habit is also commonly accompanied by other low-key movements, such as arms close to the body, a quiet voice and, sometimes, nervous, fidgety hands. Moving this way can make you appear shy, under-prepared or overwhelmed.

Walk and talk like a manager There is certainly something appealing about an interested, smart person who shows up to work confident, poised and alert. I have to say I have coached more people because they were qualified and needed coaching because they didn't walk and talk the part, rather than the other way around. Be mindful of focusing on creating an attractive combination of walking and talking for yourself. Make sure it is authentic and the best version of yourself.

Foundational movements

The challenge we face is that it is far too easy to engineer meaningful movement out of everyday life. More and more of our meetings are virtual, many of us work remotely, sitting in front of screens and devices that limit the need to move our bodies.

So how can we intentionally use movement in our body language? Movement is one of the most powerful ways we can affect tone and mood when we are in a room with others.

In any space, you can move forwards or back, side to side or up and down (standing and seated). It might not always feel that way, but you can control more in a space than you think. Combine using a specific 'place' in the room with the message you are communicating and you create a new super-power for yourself.

Be mindful that with any of these positions, the power comes from making sure your movement is congruent with and supporting your message and intent. Because the combination is so powerful, when it works, it's wonderful. If it doesn't work, it can create distraction.

Think about this: every place you go to in a room has a 'feeling' associated with it. For example, if you are standing

6 It is important for you to be just as comfortable with resting or stopping as you are with the movement itself. 9

enough distance away from the main point of focus in a room, you may be too far away from the action to feel engaged in it. If you are standing too close to someone, you may also feel some discomfort or natural tension. You know how it feels to be in a meeting, seated where it is awkward to be seen by everyone or too far away from the decision maker. My point is, everywhere you go and stand or sit in a room creates a feeling, whether you think about it or not. I suggest you consider it when it matters to you.

Effective movement relies on you starting the movement, moving confidently and definitely through the space as you arrive where you want to be, then stopping. When you are ready, move again, complete the movement and stop. The same principle applies to any aspect of body language; it is important for you to be just as comfortable with resting or stopping as you are with the movement itself. Consider the following foundational moves and positions you can take up in a room:

I've got this I'm often asked about the best way to enter and 'own a room'. I think the most important accessory is your frame of mind. Someone once said to me a long time ago as I was moaning about having to go to an after-work cocktail party, 'There's something interesting about everyone, just go and find it.' Curiosity will be your best friend in any 'entrance' you ever have to make. When you enter a room, keep your chin and chest facing forwards and shoulders relaxed and slightly back. Keep a slight space between your arms and torso and make sure your hands are visible.

Subtle purposeful action Move into the room, away from the entrance and, depending on the context, begin with a subtle purposeful action. This is defined as the first (most immediate) action you take after you enter a room – after pausing for a moment on entering and getting your bearings.

For example, if it's possible, make eye contact with colleagues or people you already know and greet them. If you don't know anyone, continue to keep your body relaxed, alert and facing forwards, chin and eyes level. Depending on the circumstances, this action can include finding your seat at the meeting table, greeting a stranger, moving to the food or drink area, greeting the host or walking up to a small cluster of people and asking to join them. It's not hard to work this out when you get into the room. A friend of mine who feels a lot of anxiety in these situations plans this movement ahead of time by agreeing to meet someone in the room, or makes an excuse to go directly to someone she knows. Checking your device doesn't count as this!

I'm imparting information This is where you are standing or seated at the front of the room and the listener's attention is focused on you. The front of the room is the most neutral and common place to start and lead a discussion, meeting or presentation. While you are standing here, the feeling you create in the room is that of teacher or guide. You are imparting information to the listener, all of the focus is on you, in the same way that a teacher stands in front of a classroom to teach. This position works particularly well when you are physically signalling you are ready to start, when you are opening or closing your meeting or presentation, or when you want to create the feeling of sharing information.

I'm guiding and facilitating This position is really powerful if you are using any visual aids or want to shift the focus of the listener away from you directly and onto your shared focus. From this position, the eyes of your listeners are on you and also the visual, with you facilitating understanding and the discussion. Be sure to stand in such a way that you are not blocking the view of the listener, and close enough so you can still create the 'feeling' of facilitator. Think about facilitating an 'energetic triangle' (see right) between you and the listener, you and the visual, and the listener and the visual. This position works particularly well when you are explaining or clarifying – and positioning yourself close to the visual is helpful.

you ⟷ visual

listener(s)

We're in this together If your subject matter would be enhanced by 'sharing the view' with your listeners, to create the feeling of looking at it together, you want to be able to move into this position without causing offence or discomfort. Be mindful of not stopping too close behind someone as you make your way around the table into this position. Stand just a little to the front and to the side of the person next to you but not too far away. Your goal is to create a feeling of partnership with them. This position is particularly powerful if you want to reinforce the feeling that, 'We are in this together', or 'Let's have a look at what we have created', or 'Let's look closer at the task ahead for us all'.

I'm with you all the way This is a very dynamic move to the back of the room while your listeners are facing forwards, towards the visual. You create the feeling that you are 'urging people on' and that you are a coach pushing the team forwards towards the goal or outcome. With this move, be sure that there is ample space and you can get to the back of the room easily, so it's worth rehearsing. I have seen it work beautifully at meetings for business leaders with big teams and big goals (and big rooms).

If you are going to move to a place, be definite about it. Then, stay there. Notice and savour how the place supports you and your message. When you are ready, move to the next best place. Stay in contact with your listeners, so either stop talking while you move to your next place or be careful not to deliver important messages to the floor as you look where you are going.

If you want to proceed step by step (no pun intended) into using movement, it's a good idea to make a movement map (see right). Build one into your content and make a note, for example, of where you might get up from the table in order to signal the beginning of the discussion or move to set up a visual, stay there a moment while facilitating the visual and then move to the centre or just off-side of centre to continue the discussion. Stay there a while, discussing some content and fielding questions, then perhaps move to facilitate from the other side of the room. Start with small, purposeful movements, using the front of the room. Teacher and facilitator are the easiest to achieve in most situations, build from there over time.

I realize it may feel a bit daunting to think about moving your body around a room, particularly if you've never thought about doing it before or realize how powerful it can be in setting the tone and mood in a room. Yes, it can

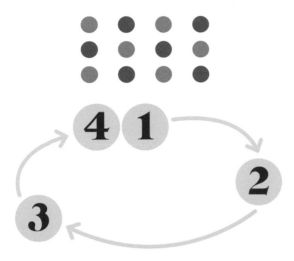

be higher risk if you are not aware of it or plan for it. Know, though, that you will create a tone and mood whether or not you think about it or plan for it. Of course, you won't be moving all the time. The point of these Foundational moves is that they are an optimal place for you to be in a room when your message calls for it. Most people don't move with intent. Rather, they move based on an unconscious energetic release (leaks), chance or when forced into moving in whatever way the room setup dictates. Foundational moves create focus and meaning for your message and give your body a chance to do what it wants to naturally.

So, as you can see, the Three Sisters of Posture, Gesture and Movement work together to support you. The integrity of your natural, balanced posture serves the congruous, creative and expressive use of your gestures, which, in turn, serves the ease of movement in more meaningful ways. Attention to one of them will make it easier for you to attend to and improve the others.

Eye Contact

3

The power in eye contact lies in two places: your ability to use it appropriately with others, in whatever context, and as a personal 'muscle-builder' to help you cultivate focus, confidence, attention, understanding and calm.

You can't fake eye contact. Well, maybe you can for a few minutes until how you really feel or think begins to reveal itself. When we make eye contact, our thoughts and emotions are closest to the surface of our skin. This is good news and bad news. If you're nervous, lacking confidence, under-prepared or doubting yourself, it is likely to show here. If you are prepared, confident, interested and grounded, it is also likely to show here.

Eye contact is a voluntary movement that improves with practise. It is as natural a body function as walking. As you become more aware of the power of eye contact, the next best step is to consider how to refine it through training.

The definition of appropriate eye contact depends on a lot of factors. How we use eye contact is reinforced by our social conditioning, how comfortable we are with it, our upbringing, and cultural and societal norms. Scientists tell us that when we make eye contact with someone, it triggers a raft of brain activity in exactly the same areas in ourselves as the other person. We also know that the brain can tell the difference between a live video call and a recorded video clip of other people making eye contact with you, even when you haven't consciously spotted the difference.

Eye contact involves specific parts of the brain, in particular the cerebellum and the limbic mirror system, which both activate when we observe someone else moving their eyes and the rest of their body in the same way. The limbic system in general is what strengthens our ability to recognize and share emotion. It is critical for our capacity to build rapport and trust, and feel empathy. These brain systems also underpin our ability to improve self-awareness. So, making eye contact is a powerful way to make sure you are not missing out on the benefits that we know human engagement can offer.

If we avoid making eye contact, our brains lose the critical cerebral fitness activity that occurs when we look in another person's eyes. This means that real-time eye contact prepares the social part of your brain to share a mental state with another person. It communicates attention of a particular kind, such as the feeling of, 'I am attending to you'. By attention, I mean your ability to observe, focus on, be mindful of or take special care of someone or something. Attention underpins effective eye contact.

The amount of eye contact to use

Just because someone uses a lot of eye contact doesn't mean, however, that they are a good communicator and the opposite is also true. So much of what works or doesn't work depends on context and the other person's comfort to engage with you.

There is no right or wrong eye contact, it depends on where you are, with whom and what you want to achieve. Just keep in mind that whatever level of eye contact you make in a particular context – a little, a lot or somewhere in between – you always have a choice.

From my experience in Western/European and many African and Latin American cultures, the common wisdom for the amount of eye contact during conversations is 60–65 per cent of the time while speaking and 75 per cent while listening. In Asia, my experience is different. Working in Japan, I had to reduce the amount of eye contact I naturally used while conversing so I wouldn't come across as too direct or disrespectful during training sessions. It was difficult for me because my culture and conditioning demand that eye contact communicates authority in my role as a coach. Not so everywhere.

Speaking and eye contact

Speaking while maintaining eye contact can feel a little awkward at times. It feels as if you are unable to search for words without releasing your gaze. There have been some studies that support that eye contact while speaking is harder because we feel self-conscious, blank out and lose our train of thought. It can feel like we need to break away from eye contact to compose ourselves or concentrate. This tends to happen more when the pressure is on you, such as during an important presentation or a difficult or confrontational situation. It is a natural response to look away but, with practise and awareness, you can neutralize the reflex of these unconscious responses.

Effective use of eye contact means being flexible and able to use more or less eye contact when you need to. One of the most beautiful truths about eye contact is that as you become more comfortable with it and more aware of how you are using it, your own feelings of self-consciousness will start to melt away. Improvement in eye contact is like an accelerant to improvement in the other aspects of body language and communication. If you can consciously improve your use of eye contact, you can do just about anything!

Default behaviours

When it comes to eye contact, default behaviours appear when the focus of your attention is not fully aligned with your intention. By that I mean there are times when it is important that your voice is heard clearly and your point is taken or your desires known, but it appears to the other person that you are not giving them your full attention. Our eye contact can become misaligned when we are in situations where we are under stress, lacking confidence or feeling self-conscious. So, what you intend to communicate doesn't come across as powerfully as it could because your eye contact (or lack thereof) communicates something else. This misalignment because of tension is compounded by a lack of awareness about how you're using your eye contact.

Let's have a look at some of the most common default behaviours in women and their use of eye contact.

Drop it like it's hot One of the most common behaviours is dropping eye contact while speaking one-on-one or to a group just before you finish making your point or a strong statement. Notice the timing. It usually drops just before the sentences are completed, at a time when your eye contact could be used powerfully to reinforce to the other person what is important to you. The gaze drops to the table or to your hands or the floor or, if you are in a presentation, to your visual aid. Your message is, in effect, tossed away when it is at its most meaningful to you and the listener.

Everything and nothing This default is eye contact that flitters everywhere while speaking but doesn't see anything. The listener may at first believe the other person is making eye contact, but the eyes are not collecting information, they are just moving – to the floor, ceiling, the spaces between people, spaces around the room – and not resting anywhere. Often the person with this default doesn't remember faces or expressions and misses nuances and direct feedback from the listener. This kind of eye contact is also associated with speaking too fast or the feeling of needing to 'catch your breath'. Another aspect of this default is the party-goer we have all met who comes to greet you but looks over your shoulder and around the room from the moment they say 'nice to meet you' and shake your hand.

Unusual, exaggerated or plain uncomfortable
This is eye contact that can be considered a distraction to the listener. The default can include using it too much (staring or a prolonged gaze) or too little; exaggerated looking up, down or side to side while talking; and unusual blinking patterns or squinting. Sometimes this default can be related to cultural expectations or personal conditioning, social anxiety or a symptom of being on the autism spectrum (see overleaf).

In most Westernized countries, eye contact is mostly welcomed without conditions between all ages and sexes. Since my work has been largely in a business context, it is safe to say that the corporate world has made an imprint on expectations

about eye contact. There are some unwritten rules to know and respect while travelling in certain countries: between opposite sexes; between elders and young people; between members of the same sex. It is difficult to generalize, so in the foundational part of this chapter, I will show you how to figure out how to use appropriate eye contact in any moment.

A recent study indicated that some people on the autism spectrum have problems maintaining eye contact because of 'excessive arousal' that is triggered in their brains. My clients who have identified as being on the autism spectrum all stated eye contact as being very uncomfortable for them. For many people there is some level of social anxiety associated with eye contact. I promise that for most of you who feel extreme discomfort, you shouldn't despair! If you find that your discomfort is to the point that looking someone in the eye is overly distressing, seek help from a mental health professional or your family doctor, where your symptoms will be assessed and a treatment plan for your unique situation developed.

Foundational eye contact

Remember that when you are communicating, you are always only ever communicating with one person at a time. By that I mean every individual with whom you communicate, either one-on-one or a participant in a large group, will leave an encounter with you knowing only what it meant to them. They will decide if they 'got what they came for', were satisfied and enthusiastic, intrigued or indifferent.

❝ I have learned that people will forget what you said, forget what you did, but will never forget how you made them feel. ❞ Maya Angelou

Even with the best intentions, communication can sometimes be hit-and-miss. We can reduce the odds of mishap dramatically through thorough preparation and as importantly, how you communicate your message. How you communicate is where eye contact punches above its weight.

Earlier in this chapter, I referred to eye contact as being a kind of attention and how it prepares your brain to share a mental state with another person. Imagine attention as a pie that can be divided and served up as you want or need to. The pie is delicious to most people and you have an endless supply. As you get more demands on your attention, you get more pie.

In work and socially, you communicate both one-on-one and to groups. Certain people are more important to you than others at different times. For example, if you are making a presentation or running a meeting, there may be specific individuals whom you are called upon to influence and persuade. At other times, your role may just be to inform people or be an expert on a subject. There is a link between how important someone is to your success and wellbeing and the amount of eye contact and attention they receive from you.

One-on-one eye contact

Research shows us that most people are comfortable with three to four seconds of eye contact during conversations with strangers, a little more if the stranger seems trustworthy. The truth is you don't always know right away how someone feels about engaging with you or how comfortable they are with eye contact.

Start the same, then increase

Using a 'start the same, then increase' approach allows you to be flexible and at greater ease in most one-on-one situations. First, notice how comfortable the other person is with eye contact, pay attention to their cues and then gently match them. They may become more talkative, use more eye contact and participate more in the conversation. If they don't begin to increase their eye contact with you, be patient and continue to match theirs. This strategy will serve you most of the time in one-on-one situations. If someone starts out too strong with you and you are uncomfortable, don't be compelled to match their eye contact. You'll know when you don't want to. If the 'start the same, then increase' approach is working, you can follow the 50/70 general guideline: maintain eye contact 50 per cent of the time when speaking and 70 per cent when listening.

At first, try holding eye contact for five to six seconds at a time and graduate to using more qualitative eye contact that is linked to what you are saying. This means using eye contact both for effect and to reinforce meaning and importance. In other words, hold eye contact during complete sentences and when making important points, and during pauses.

It's natural to feel a need to look away. When you do, do it slowly and deliberately. Darting your eyes away quickly can make you appear nervous, shy or shifty. When you break eye contact, glance to the side gently before resuming your gaze. You can also break your gaze with a purpose by using a gesture or a nod or while you are note-taking (looking at your device doesn't count!).

A tip some of my students love is, rather than looking away, you take a break on another aspect of their face. Imagine an inverted triangle connecting the eyes and mouth. As you need to, rotate your gaze around the imaginary triangle. Perhaps linger on one eye at a time, then the mouth. This triangle technique gives a short-term reprieve from genuine eye contact, so I'd like you to use it only sparingly.

Getting stronger

One of my favourite techniques is to make eye contact for two or three seconds before speaking. It engages your attention – and theirs. Also, try holding your gaze for two or three seconds after you finish speaking. This is a real attention muscle-builder as it forces you to stay engaged during the important moments when you may feel like disengaging.

Large and small groups

I mentioned earlier that you only ever have an audience of one. People will decide whether what you said or did is relevant or makes sense to them. Adding an eye contact strategy to your knowledge of how your listeners will be impacted is a powerful mix. Here are four strategies to use depending on your situation.

1. Knowing the decision makers Sometimes you will be in a meeting or a situation with a group of people you need to persuade; some may be decision makers, some may be influencing the decision. Each person should get the right amount of the right eye contact attention depending on how they will be impacted by your message.

If someone is a decision maker, they need 60 per cent plus of your eye contact and attention. It means that you know who the decision maker is and what information needs to be directed at them, and when. The information that needs to be communicated to decision-makers is often the critical meat of your message and it doesn't make sense to focus on the wrong person.

I have been in situations where I was the decision maker, but because the person communicating hadn't done their homework, they were focusing their attention on the wrong person about critical decision-making factors for which I was responsible. If you have ever been a decision maker and been left out of the focus on the issues relevant to your decision, you know how it feels.

2. Being aware of the key influencers You may also face circumstances where there are also key influencers in the room and they need the next largest slice of your eye contact. These are the people who will often make or break the final decision as they will be relied upon by someone to execute an aspect of your recommendation or support the ultimate decision in some way. It is up to you to recognize this, know who influences what and how, and then divide your eye contact accordingly.

3. Everyone is equal There are times when the individuals in the meeting or conversation are colleagues, peers or partners. Everyone is equal is a strategy you may use if you are in a situation where, in fact, everyone is equal and there is no benefit to dividing your attention as if there were differences in power between people. Eye contact is, in effect, divided equally to all present. This is also a go-to strategy if you don't have information about where the power lies or how the decision will be made. When dividing eye contact equally at first, I have noticed that if there are decision makers and influencers present, they will soon make themselves known.

To divide attention equally around a room, you need to be careful not to be mechanical – for example, moving from one person to the next in a predictable clock-like order or moving your eyes in a zigzag fashion, as if lacing a shoe. This is unnatural for you and it becomes distracting for the listener. The audience of one, which I mentioned earlier, applies here, too. You need to make sufficient eye contact with the individuals present for them to feel like you are treating them all as equals, while keeping in mind that everyone may be a little different in their comfort levels.

Think of grapes. Think of groups of people as existing in clusters, like a small handful of grapes. It is natural for you to make genuine eye contact with individuals in clusters of two or three, or five or six at a time, in a cluster, rather than trying to make eye contact with everyone, all at once. So, at your meeting table, or with a small or large group gathered, engage with one cluster at a time. Move your eye contact to an individual and two or three people near them. Complete your thought, then move to the next individual and their cluster. Avoid sharp moves to the right or left, or mechanically like a clock around the table or room.

4. Public speaking Take this clustering technique to public speaking. Now you are in a larger room full of people but they are still individuals who need to feel like you are communicating to them as individuals and clustering helps you do this. Because of the proximity realities of a public speaking space (mostly the distance between you and your listener), to achieve the same intimacy as in a smaller space, you need to exaggerate a little in order that people see you. For example, just moving your eyeballs to an individual off to the right or left is too subtle to be seen by your listener, which it would be in a smaller space. In order to really communicate and make eye contact with them, you need to think about clusters.

The good news about public speaking is that because of the distance between you and the listener, when you make eye contact with an individual, that person and five or six individuals immediately next to them feel like they are also getting eye contact. An instant cluster! You address that individual cluster to share a thought or make a point, and move gently to another cluster around the room. Avoid mechanically zigzagging or sweeping from side to side with your eye contact. Instead, engage a cluster, face them gently with your body as if speaking only to them, move to another cluster, gently facing them, move to another cluster and so on, targeting your attention to the middle, sides, forward and back of the room. Your goal is to create a feeling of engaging individuals in the whole room, one cluster at a time. As your audience watches you engage individuals, you create the feeling overall of a conversation between you and your listeners. (In contrast, you may have seen speakers use eye contact that appears to be directed theatrically to the back of the room or sweeping from side to side as if their message is being sprayed out of a hose.) It takes a little practise, but once you get the feel for it, even a big room can become a small one.

Improving the quality of your eye contact will improve your ability to pay attention and the quality of that attention. It will also boost your self-awareness, boost your feeling of confidence under pressure and accelerate other body language improvements you may be exploring.

Practising eye contact

The exercises opposite will help you practise and refine your eye contact. Some of them require you to recruit a friend or a few friends. If you want to practise without having to recruit anyone, a good way to start is by increasing daily eye contact with people you know, such as family members and friends. I have found another good way to improve is to try to make more eye contact with people who are providing you with a service, such as your server in a restaurant or a cashier at the supermarket. In this way, you will gradually build your comfort and confidence.

My colleagues and I have been conducting the exercises opposite with clients for decades to help them build confidence, resilience and gravitas. They are intense and exaggerated, but designed to help you become more aware of your own comfort level with eye contact and to gradually develop flexibility using eye contact in a range of situations. These exercises are not about you learning to stare at people. Rather, they are about you becoming more comfortable with looking and being looked at, and sitting with the discomfort this can bring. It will get easier with practise. I recommend doing these exercises in the privacy of your home or office.

One-on-one seated silent Find someone you know to work with. Sit in a chair across from them, feet flat on the floor, knees almost touching. Relax your shoulders, rest your hands in your lap and breathe normally. Set the timer for two minutes. No talking.

1. Look at your partner, moving your eyes gently on their face from one eye to the other eye only, but nowhere else on the face. You may feel uncomfortable or start to laugh, or want to talk. This is normal. Just keep breathing, recentre yourself, regain eye contact and maintain silence. If you need to look away, do so and come back to the exercise gently when you are ready.

2. Continue for the full two minutes. Build to three minutes if you can. Repeat three times with a small break in between exercises. When you are finished, thank your partner.

How did it feel? What did you notice about the experience? There is no right or wrong answer.

One-on-one seated speaking Begin as above. The point of this exercise is to practise improving your full eye contact while answering a question.

1. You and your partner choose 'five things' for the other person to name – such as five favourite foods, five famous movies or five current events. The exercise should last for approximately three to five minutes.

2. Face each other with full eye contact. Decide who starts and when to begin, and from that point, no matter how difficult, maintain eye contact while asking or answering. Complete two rounds of questions and answers for each person. Don't tell your partner your questions before the exercise.

You will notice it is hard to maintain full eye contact while searching for an answer to a question. This is an exercise to raise your awareness of how you may unconsciously be using eye contact while under pressure. How did it feel? What did you notice about the experience? There is no right or wrong answer.

Group eye contact, standing silent This exercise is for three people but can be extended to ten.

1. Begin with one person standing at the front of the room or at the head of a table. Everyone seated makes eye contact with the person standing. The person standing begins by making eye contact with one person and holds that for approximately ten seconds. The seated person engages the standing person by making eye contact. Everyone around the table continues to look at the standing person.

2. The standing person then gently moves their eye contact (gaze) to another person seated at the table and holds that for approximately ten seconds. The seated person engages the standing person by making eye contact.

3. The standing person then gently moves their eye contact (gaze) to the third and final seated person and holds for approximately ten seconds. The seated person engages the standing person by making eye contact.

4. After the third person has been engaged, the standing person can sit down at the table and the next person comes to the front of the room. Repeat until everyone has had a chance to participate. How did it feel? What did you notice about the experience? There is no right or wrong answer.

Group eye contact, standing speaking This exercise is for three people but can be extended to ten. The goal is for the person standing to speak only when they have full eye contact with individuals in the audience. If you need to look away, stop talking. You can add an extra challenge of facilitating a visual aid such as a flip chart or projected image on a screen.

This exercise is exaggerated but designed to help you become more aware of how much effort is needed to maintain eye contact with your listeners while speaking. For most people, there is little awareness that most of their eye contact is given to the floor, furniture, visual aids or somewhere in between. How did it feel? What did you notice about the experience? There is no right or wrong answer.

Voice and Facial Expression

Our facial expressions and voice work together to help us communicate feelings and emotion. They act as a powerful reality double-check on each other. Even though they live and work closely together and most of the time complement each other, they still operate with separate brain functions and deserve their own separate sections in this chapter.

When we are chatting with our friends, most of us believe that we rely on facial expression to read how others are feeling. However, science tells us that we overestimate our ability to understand other people's emotions through their facial expressions. In a study that measured the accuracy of listening to both the voice and seeing facial expressions, our interpretations are more accurate without the visual distraction of the face. We are better at perceiving emotional nuances when our full attention is focused just on the voice.

It appears that this is because we can detect a wider range of emotions through the voice, such as positivity, negativity, calm, as well as detecting more nuanced emotions, which can include distinguishing fear from anger and embarrassment from shyness.

When the emotion is expressed through your voice and it doesn't match the one sent by the expression on your face, our brains will give priority to the visual message, not to the auditory one, and we sense a lie. Of course, maybe that person may not have meant to mislead you but, rather, could be embarrassed about making a fool of themselves. However, our brain registers the mismatch.

So, your face will trump your voice when they are used together. But without your face in the picture, your voice will give your listener a better idea of how you feel.

I'm not saying that the facial expression component is less important – expressions are vital for understanding what someone is feeling or thinking. Different parts of our brain are activated when receiving facial expression and voice information.

Voice

Our voices are as distinctive as our faces. Physically, your voice is supported by a complex structure of cartilage, ligaments and muscle. If you reach up and gently feel the shapes, the texture and warmth of your throat and neck, you'll notice some of it is strong and supple, other parts thinner and sinewy. Notice how your throat and the area around it change when your vocal cords vibrate as you speak, sing, shout or whisper. Your diaphragm, located at the base of your chest, is a hardworking friend of your voice, whose main job is to ensure you can move the right amount of oxygen in and out of your body. Your healthy and natural voice involves a collaboration that includes your breath and your whole body, from head to toe.

Your voice is also strongly tied to your personal identity. In everyday life, your voice has the power to completely change the way others perceive you and it is an important element in evoking what you want from other people. In Western culture, in particular, there has been a feeling among women that finding the 'right' voice could somehow unlock opportunity more easily. Research suggests that due to a sense of changing power dynamics between men and women, the pitch of women's voices dropped considerably in the second half of the last century. As women have risen to more prominent roles in society, they have adopted a lower and deeper tone to their voice, thereby, allegedly, projecting more authority and dominance in the workplace.

I have spent 30 years working with women who were given feedback that their voices were 'too' something: loud, girly, squeaky, nasal, breathy, matronly, whispered. It was hard to hear this without feeling that what this feedback implied was that the voices were lacking in power, humour, softness, warmth, seriousness, coolness or intellect. I noticed these characteristics did not accurately describe the women I met and coached. However, while the misperception is frustrating, impressions don't have to be right to matter. The good news is that you can find the balance of what feels natural to you and what's needed to get your message across to your listener through awareness and training.

Default behaviours

How people perceive the character of your voice involves not only what you say but how you say it: how loudly, quickly or clearly you speak; the resonance of your voice; the use of inflection; the clarity and strength of your voice. And, in more subtle ways, even how you use silence. Let's look at some of the most common default behaviours that involve your voice.

Speaking up How you use your voice is influenced by your culture, family, circumstances and your physical structure. The key to getting your voice to work for you is to think of what I like to refer to as 'speaking up'. By that I mean being able to adjust your voice so that it accurately represents how you feel and what you mean, in a way that serves you best in a particular context. In other words, your voice is calculated and calibrated to be in tune with your listener and what you want to achieve.

Women are often given feedback that their voices should be louder and have a more confident tone. We can get stuck in a vocal comfort zone that has the same tone and volume as a conversation, which doesn't always serve us. I have noticed that many women don't use vocal tone or volume in a way that reflects their status, experience or expertise. Instead, they withhold their contributions, or downplay or apologize for them. My colleague Martha, who coaches business leaders in New York City, refers to women's voices as having 'retreated down back inside themselves' due to poor socialization and conditioning. There is a long history of women silencing themselves in order to defer, not to frighten or offend, but to be comforting and pleasant.

I want you to think about speaking up as our kind of velvet rebellion – a non-violent transition of power, every day in every way.

Discomfort with silence When we are not comfortable with silence, one of the common ways we react is to use 'fillers'. These are words, sounds and other vocal actions that distract us from what feels like a scary silent abyss between words or thoughts. We are not always conscious of how many filler words we are using until someone points it out to us or we hear a recording of ourselves. You really feel the presence of the fillers when you try to stop using them.

'kind of'

'like'

'err'

Fillers include words such as: like, you know, right, really, I think, I'm sorry, maybe, I believe, pretty much, kind of, sort of; and sounds such as: umm, errr, ahh; or nervous or inappropriate chatter or laughter. Fillers can also be disguised as interrupting and talking over someone, responding quickly without thinking, jumping in to advise before an issue is clarified or monopolizing airspace. The challenge with fillers is that when you use them, they impact your ability to listen fully. You stop registering what is going on around you and miss clues from your listeners. It can also make you sound monotone and unsure of yourself. Additionally, fillers can affect clarity and create distraction for your listener because of the tendency to string words together and speak too quickly.

Have you ever been in a situation when you asked someone a question and, as the listener struggled with their answer, you jumped in and started speaking or changed the subject because the silence made you uncomfortable? Perhaps you were the person being asked a question and felt self-conscious about the silence required to formulate your thoughts and then started thinking out loud to fill the space?

Different communication styles discussed in Chapter 2 also reflect different levels of comfort with silence. People who are more Expressive find it difficult to stay silent, whereas Analytical people easily feel silence can be part of the process of finding a solution. Often, we need only a few more seconds of silence on both sides for clarity to emerge.

Framing, apologizing and uptalk

We have probably all heard that it's not what you say but how you say it. That's partly true, and when it comes to framing, apologizing and uptalk, the how and the what come together as one. Let me explain what I mean by these terms.

'Framing' refers to the effect you have on others by the way you set up, present or explain something to someone. For example, imagine someone wanting to perform surgery on you and they say that it has a 90 per cent chance of survival. Pretty good, right? If they framed it differently, saying the surgery has a 10 per cent chance of death, your reaction would probably be different. This is because of cognitive bias. It means we are likely to feel better when something is presented to us in a positive way, or in a way that benefits us, rather than in a way with a negative frame.

I often hear women negatively framing their comments and suggestions by slipping negative frames into their responses or stories, such as, 'I'm not sure if this is the right approach' or 'Someone else might have a different view on this', 'I'm not an expert on this' or 'I may not be the right person to have this opinion', 'Some of you may disagree with me', 'May I just say'. These negative frames set up an emotional response in others that feels like regret for what you are about to say, or unworthiness and an apology for the mere fact that you are speaking up.

Apologizing is using the word 'sorry' both before or after something has happened, whether it was called for or not, such as 'Forgive me for interjecting' and 'Sorry, may I say something here?'. 'Sorry' or 'Excuse me' can certainly be a form of good manners in the right context, but if it becomes something you say without thinking, it becomes an unconscious frame that communicates, 'It's my fault, regardless'.

Uptalk is common among certain women in mostly English-speaking countries or where English is a second language. It refers to a pattern where you inflect a sentence to sound like a question (you know, like this?). Some argue that this kind of inflection has the effect of inviting the listener to listen actively and to nod and confirm more often because your speech pattern has turned every statement into a question. But it can also have the effect of making you sound unsure. My experience is that uptalk is also a big distraction to you, the speaker. Uptalk is a pattern that erases variety and emphasis from your voice and makes it unclear what you think is important or urgent about your message.

If you are not sure if you uptalk, record yourself and listen. Rehearse and repeat some of the phrases by ending with a flat or downwards inflection, like making a statement or a declaration. Listen again. Start by making changes with small talk with friends and family and build up to full conversations. One of my students in her final project decided to tackle her uptalk while making a daily video journal. She told me she had to re-record the video several times to finally conquer the problem! It was a helpful learning experience.

Foundational voice

The foundational voice practice is a way to support your speaking voice over a healthy lifetime of use, and also to help you find your own personal best quality voice that represents you authentically in a range of situations.

Projecting your best-quality voice

Getting your voice 'right' can be a precarious and frustrating path to follow. We have some measure of control over how we sound, but chasing labels like 'authoritative' or 'competent' or 'neutral' is subjective and varies according to the individual and culture. You'll soon realize that everyone has an imagined standard to defend. If we were to create an equation for a person's unique voice, it could look something like this:

Voice quality =
- how your vocal tract is configured
- + anatomy of your larynx
- + learned behaviour (vocal habits)

In other words, it is partly genetic, partly learned. Yet there is still disagreement about the exact descriptions of voice qualities. We can talk forever about what makes someone attractive but we don't really have a common language to describe vocal quality. You recognize it when you hear it.

According to researchers in the field of vocology, there are some agreed-upon descriptions of certain vocal qualities, how they are perceived and how one's physiology creates them. This is a partial list of terms suggested by Dr Ingo Titze, vocologist extraordinare and executive director of the National Center for Voice and Speech in Utah. The list is by no means complete, but here are some of the most common vocal qualities I recognize in women:

Voice Quality / Perception

Diplophonic
pitch is one octave lower, with a roughness (vocal fry)

Resonant
brightened or 'ringing' sound that carries well with ease and vibrancy

Breathy
sound of air is apparent

Strained
effort in the voice, overuse of neck muscles

Hoarse (raspy)
harsh, grating sound

Honky
excessive nasality

Tremulous
affected by nervousness, uncertainty or fear

Dr Titze says that our entire personality, mood, health and heritage are encoded in our voice and tell us a lot about an individual, in the moment.

I want you to find your vocal sweet spot. By that I mean cultivating the skills to build the strength to be flexible, exercise a wider variety of natural capabilities already built into your voice and to be able to call upon the voice that is uniquely you and adaptable to suit the context in which you find yourself.

The tension we carry in our bodies can affect our overall wellbeing and the voice is particularly affected by this. We all store tension differently. You know where yours is! Perhaps your neck, shoulders, hips, upper or lower back, or jaw? Unless this tension is eased, your voice cannot fully function. Your sweet spot is blocked.

Professional speakers, actors and singers prioritize relaxing the whole body before their vocal 'warm-up'. Relaxation helps you focus your energy exactly where it needs to be. I have included relaxation, vocal warm-up and general vocal health exercises in this chapter. All of the exercises will help you protect and cultivate your natural voice. It all starts with mastering relaxation.

After relaxation, I believe that the best place to continue the journey for your sweet spot is to focus on learning to project your best quality voice. By that I mean to speak so your listener can hear you and to do so in a way that feels to the listener that it was directed to them with the greatest ease and authenticity on your part.

Voice projection

A good, quick test for your own voice projection is to begin by holding your hand about 5 cm (2 in) from your mouth, palm facing in, and speak normally. Try to feel your breath on your hand as you speak.

Then move your hand 15–18 cm (6–7 in) from your mouth and continue to speak. You may need to speak up a little and push the breath to still be able to feel it. Now extend your hand out to arm's length and project as if you needed to be heard at the back of the room. Do you feel what your body has to do at each different level of voice projection? It's easy to feel the breath when your hand is close to the mouth. If it's 15–18 cm (6–7 in) away, you need to speak a little louder and more consciously push the breath and more deliberately shape your words to feel it on your hand. Change happens again when you need to reach the back of the room. Think about the last word in your sentence and use the same amount of breath as your first.

Your best quality voice is affected greatly by your level of confidence in what you're saying and your intention to communicate. If you mean what you're saying deep in your heart, know it and want it, and your communication will be actively directed TO someone. The quality of your voice reflects it.

Relaxation for projection and resonance

Projection and resonance stem from the breath and relaxation. This means that you breathe fully and relax the tension in your body from head to toe. Kristin Linklater, a global icon in the world of voice coaching, said, 'If you are holding your breath in any way, part of you is absent.'

We all hold onto our own brand of tension in ways that restrict our breathing and movement to some degree. Here are some exercises that will help you with building your base for projection and resonance.

1. Find a quiet place free from distractions. Lie down or sit in a chair, arms relaxed in your lap. Loosen any tight clothing and remove your glasses.

2. Take a few slow, even breaths. Let your body relax into the floor or the chair, feeling the gentle pull of gravity.

3. Begin by focusing your attention on your forehead, jaw, lips, temple, chin. Let them totally relax and drop. Let your tongue release from the roof of your mouth. Leave the rest of your body relaxed and begin to gently massage the facial area with small, gentle circular motions. Continue to release the tension, being careful not to press too hard on the face while massaging. Continue breathing slowly and evenly.

4. Now shift your attention to your neck and shoulders. Raise your shoulders up towards your ears and hold for 15 seconds. Slowly release the tension as you count for 30 seconds. Notice any tension melting away.

5. If you can, gently raise one arm, gently stretching up high while taking a gentle deep breath, exhaling with the mouth open. Now do the other side. Repeat if it feels good.

6. After a moment of rest, focus your attention on your arms and hands. Make a fist with each hand, and draw your arms into your chest and hold

for 15 seconds as tightly as you can, then release the tension for 30 seconds. Notice a feeling of relaxation.

7. Gently increase the tension in your buttocks and upper thighs. Squeeze tightly for 15 seconds and release for 30 seconds.

8. Move to your feet. Slowly tighten the muscles in your toes and feet for 15 seconds and release for 30 seconds. Continue to breathe slowly and evenly.

9. Notice the sensation of relaxation in your body. Stay there a few moments, noticing your breathing.

Breathing practice

Find a quiet place, free of distractions. Lie on the floor or recline in a chair. Rest your hands gently in your lap or at your sides.

Place one hand on your upper chest and one on your abdomen. Inhale, take a deep gentle breath from your abdomen as you count to three. As you inhale, you should feel your stomach rise up. Focus on your abdomen and try to keep your chest from rising up. After a short pause, exhale slowly. If it helps, you can count in your mind the number of seconds per breath: inhale, 'one, two, three'; exhale, 'one, two, three'.

My personal favourite is inspired by a quote from Thich Nhat Hanh: 'Sometimes your joy is the source of your smile, but sometimes your smile is the source of your joy.'

'I Breathe In, I'm Calm'... 'I Breathe Out, I Smile.' As you breathe out, put a gentle suggestion of a smile on your face. Continue this pattern of rhythmic breathing for three to ten minutes or until you feel relaxed.

ooooooh

wwaaaaa

neeeee

Voice exercises

You can develop the quality of your voice so that it conveys a sense of warmth, competence, clarity, dynamism and an impression of force and strength (without being overly loud).

Voice warm-up and relaxation If you do any voice exercises, do them in sessions of a maximum of three to five minutes and spaced throughout the day. Don't overdo it.

1. Standing or seated, begin by noticing any tension in your face, neck and shoulders. Gently massage the face, neck and throat area. Stop, breathe gently and put your hands at your sides or in your lap.

2. Yawn, open your mouth wide, make the yawn a noisy one – say ho-hum and hold the hummmm as you wiggle your jaw from side to side with your lips and jaw loose.

3. Repeat the humming and yawning. Notice how your throat muscles have relaxed.

4. Breathe deeply, relaxing the shoulders. Open your mouth wide, loosen your jaw, exaggerate the sounds **ooooooh, wwaaaaaaa, ooooommmmm, waaaaaaaa, oooooooommm**, opening and closing the mouth and jaw slowly and deliberately. Relax your throat, yawn again, rest. Stretch your body in a way that feels comfortable. If you feel like

it, make the sounds **neeee, nooooo, nahhhhh**, relaxing the jaw.

5. Gently knead and massage your throat muscles. Relax your shoulders.

Lip trill and blowing raspberries Inhale and then blow air out of your lips from your diaphragm (not your mouth) with your lips relaxed and vibrating freely as the air passes through them.

Tongue stretch Double your tongue against your palette as far as you can, then stretch it out of your mouth as far as you can. Repeat five or six times.

Push your tongue hard against one cheek, then the other. Push it up over your upper lip and then down over your lower lip. Waggle it back and forth several times. Rest and repeat five or six times.

Stick your tongue out, make five or six circles in one direction, then reverse the direction.

While resting or speaking, let the tongue sit in its base in the lower jaw. Try to keep it from settling in the roof of your mouth. If you notice yourself pushing the tongue up into the roof, relax it and let it rest in your lower jaw.

ooommm

nahhhhh

Slowing down or speeding up your WPM
People who speak quickly generally speak at 190 words per minute, while for those who speak slowly, it's 120 words per minute. A good way to test your speed is to read out loud for a few minutes, then

divide the total number of words by the number of minutes to get your words per minute (WPM). Generally speaking, presentations should be about 100–150 WPM, conversations 120–150 WPM, audiobooks/video commentary 150–160 WPM, the most popular TED Talks 173 WPM.

To vary your speaking rate in any way, you need to be aware of the factors that may be affecting you such as your culture and conditioning (family, friends, upbringing, speaking in another language); nervousness or fatigue; complexity of the words or content and your comfort with silence.

Find a paragraph from a book or magazine. Time yourself reading it out loud and calculate your WPM. Then read it again, experimenting with varying the speed and emphasis. Practise varying your pauses as well – this means the periods of silence between words and phrases that you use to separate ideas, emphasize and hold attention. If you prefer, take selections from books, newspapers and magazines. Once you start experimenting with variations, you will become more confident applying them.

Pitch

There are four different pitch changes that you can make between words. The arrows indicate whether the voice goes up, down or remains level in the example:

No change in inflection	→	MARY
Rising up	↗	MARY
Lowering down	↘	MARY
Down and up	↝	MARY
Up and down	↜	MARY

Now try the following words and sentences and change the pitch as indicated:

Hello	→	Hello	↗
How are you?	↝	How are you?	↝
Yes	↗	Yes	↝
No	↘	No	↗

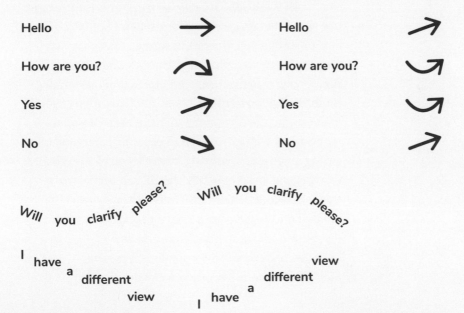

Facial Expression

We all make snap judgements about other people based on their faces. However, these snap judgements are notoriously unreliable. We make them in fractions of a second, even from just a photograph, but we have only a random chance of being right.

Across cultures, we are consistent about the 'criteria' we use to make these judgements. This includes facial cues like familiarity (whether they look like someone we know, or a vague sense of looking like someone with whom we are comfortable), fitness (whether the face is symmetrical and proportional) and emotional resemblance (whether the face resembles an emotion; whether they have naturally low-set eyebrows that make them appear angry when they are not, or an eye shape that makes them look sad or happy).

Sometimes the interpretations can become insidious. For example, *The New York Times* brought the popular culture term and internet meme 'Resting Bitch Face' (RBF) to the mainstream. This stems from women's facial expressions that appear to reveal their emotions or thoughts while they are just listening or sitting quietly. Thankfully, I was relieved to learn many of my clients based outside the US had not heard of this term. Nonetheless, RBF refers to an expression created on a resting female face that creates a distraction for some people around her.

If you understand how you form your own judgements about people, you can avoid pitfalls

'With resting calm attention face your body will actually be calmer and more easily attentive. '

and guide them to your own advantage. Also, with increased awareness about your own face and what it may communicate to others, you can begin to experience benefits immediately with small adjustments to your own facial expressions.

Facial expression defaults

Facial expression defaults are those expressions that combine your natural facial features with how you are consciously or unconsciously feeling – it may even be a way that you are trying to force yourself to feel in the moment. This mismatch between how you feel and a forced attitude in your expression is where the default appears.

These are two of the most common facial defaults I have observed:

Happy supportive face I think the world could actually use more happy, supportive faces, so don't get me wrong. HSF is wonderful except when it isn't. It is such a good feeling to see a happy and supportive face in a crowd or during a difficult situation and discover it is an authentic message to you. Be mindful not to dilute its power by overusing it.

In a negotiation recently, I was on the receiving end of a tactic that involved one of my opponents who had a supportive, smiling face. I felt distracted and confused about what was happening because I knew the discussion wasn't going well. I learned later that she was peripheral to the negotiation with no interest in the outcome. Often the friendliest face in the room is not the one with the most power or the one making the decisions around a negotiating table.

Sometimes the HSF is a sign of tension, which can make the smile and facial features look strained and make you appear nervous. At other times, this expression can come across as mockery, rudeness or cynicism.

It's over before it starts face This resting expression ranges from appearing angry, sad, doubtful, resigned, distracted, tuned-out, confused or anxious. When I have approached women privately and asked about these facial expressions, I have received such comments as, 'I didn't know I was doing that'; 'Nothing I say will make a difference, so why bother?'; 'I am a bit tired and also a bit bored with this person so I'll just listen politely until it's over'; 'I didn't prepare for this meeting and I have no idea what is supposed to happen here, so I'll keep my mouth shut'; 'I'm just going to sit here and say nothing unless I know I can answer perfectly'; 'I know this topic really well but my ideas are not taken seriously'. Whatever the case, if your resting face communicates distress or disinterest, it may or may not be what you intend but it is what people are seeing and interpreting as your current reality.

From my work with trial lawyers and juries, I know that people are less likely to find friendly faces guilty of crimes, and people who look happy are perceived to be more trustworthy, too. People tend to focus on your face as they listen, and you need to be aware of how you come across as you speak.

Foundational facial expressions

This foundational facial expression will allow you to balance between a forced, affected expression and the expression of how you really feel. By engaging in a Resting Calm Attention expression, your body will actually become calmer and more easily attentive – ready to respond in any way you need to. Your listener will also become calmer and less distracted by an impression you may be unconsciously creating.

Resting attention face Resting Attention Face reflects a calm expression of paying attention. It means you look at ease and comfortable with no visible tension. The idea is that you appear attentive without revealing obvious emotion, neither smiling nor frowning.

To achieve RAF, begin by relaxing the neck and shoulders, not slouching – think aligned and alert. Now try parting your lips slightly, no more than 6 mm (¼ in), and breathe through your mouth and nose. When your lips are slightly parted, it is harder to chew on one lip, and they can't tense, scowl or tuck.

Next, be aware of your forehead and brow. Many of us hold tension here and when we concentrate, the

calm

aligned

comfortable

alert

clear

attentive

natural

relaxed

muscles get tense in the upper part of the face and between the eyebrows. When the eyebrows get drawn together, creating a 'furrowed brow', you can appear angry or annoyed. If you feel this happening, gently move the muscles in your forehead in the opposite direction. If you lift your eyebrows slightly, the tension disappears. Lift your brows gently when you sense that your forehead and brows are tense. Have a look in the mirror to see this subtle effect.

By moving your mouth and forehead slightly, your resting face looks attentive yet calm – neither scowling nor artificially happy. The point of RAF is that by practising it, you can begin to become more aware of personal habitual internal tensions that appear in your facial expression. By replacing the expression, you make way for clearer thinking.

Keep in mind the contradiction that your efforts to remove distraction from your own expression don't change the fact that you can't always judge people by their expressions. In conversations, you get constant, subtle feedback from people as they listen and speak. They nod, smile, raise their eyebrows, frown and may make active little noises that let you know they are listening. Other people may be harder to read, either they are deliberately stone-faced or have distracting quirks of their own. Don't let this be off-putting. My goal is to help you rise above the distraction and press on.

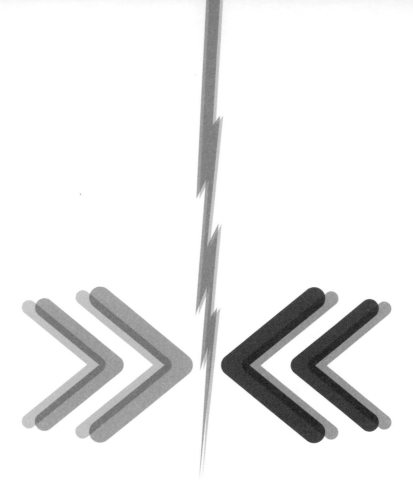

Confrontation

It's never too late for women to stand up for themselves but that's not easy when we are taught that diplomacy is the right way and that confrontation is the harsh and avoidable way. Sometimes it seems we must choose between being genuinely heard or blatantly sidelined – all for the sake of getting along.

I sincerely believe that cooperation is the way to go. But when we're up against people who are unwilling to cooperate, trying to discuss a situation that they're either going to dismiss or bully their way through, then the only answer is a juicy dose of confrontation.

In the last ten years, there has been some groundbreaking research about conflict, stress and gender differences. One of the key findings was that the old psychology of believing that male and female brains were the same when it comes to fight or flight in conflict situations was actually wrong. It's men who tend to do fight or flight, while women have a greater propensity to tend and befriend. In other words, when the going gets tough, women gravitate towards showing care and connection behaviours that support social connection.

The research showed that stress in women doesn't only motivate self-defence but also unleashes an instinct to protect your tribe. Think about it as a biological state engineered to reduce fear and increase hope.

The tend-and-befriend stress response releases the hormone oxytocin, which lessens the fight-or-flight response and prompts us to protect and gather with others. Oxytocin is considered to mediate the fight-or flight-response biologically; it is the main neurohormone responsible for social behaviours and empathy.

While men can, of course, also tend and befriend, our friend oestrogen seems to enhance it for women. Women also have a more developed prefrontal cortex, which is the consequential thinking part of the brain that also manages the amygdala, the fight-or-flight part that triggers aggression and action.

The key is women's stress response has an interesting mediator. It's not that we don't get stressed, angry and scared out of our minds but that when we're in that state, we are built to trigger the biology of courage and hope. I'm excited about what this means for our ability to deal effectively with confrontation. In my view, we have a special superpower that is underutilized for modern confrontation purposes. Our female brains facilitate our efforts to:

- Read facial expressions and take the emotional temperature of a situation

- Process details quickly

- Notice things about our environment and quickly create awareness and insight

- Bounce back and forth easily between feelings and facts

- Think holistically, allowing for the connection of new ideas and quality contextualizing

- De-stress when we can collaborate or share with others.

This is great but, as ever, having a tendency towards a hard-wired superpower has a downside. If you are not mindful of it, our ability to gather and process insight, read our environments and think holistically can sometimes bog down decision-making. I'm not too worried about that, though, because decision-making is a learned skill. However, I do get concerned that because of the way our bodies process and balance stress hormones, we can create an unhealthy stress-cycle for ourselves by getting too 'busy' with our work and personal lives that we go beyond our ability to relax and de-stress. Enter opportunity for effective confrontation with more ease and confidence.

Our brains as women are hardwired to stand strong, protect, connect and make peace. For many of us, the prospect of confrontation appears more painful than the situations themselves. I have come across intelligent, talented women whose fear of what 'someone might say' or of a possible reaction they can't handle has kept them from doing something they would really like to do. Be comforted with the knowledge that, if handled sensitively, confrontation can be both a positive and a rewarding experience.

The popular perception is that, where confrontation is concerned, women are seen to be more emotional and indirect, and actively avoid confrontation. However, many women do show aggression and comfort with displays of power, to-the-point interactions and a commanding physical presence.

Like the communication styles discussed in the previous chapter, our individual approach to confrontation represents a set of behaviours that reflects our conditioning and comfort zones. In other words, when faced with a confrontational situation, we have our own typical way of responding. Ideally, we do what we need to do, depending on the context and circumstances rather than respond the same way. I am interested in your ability to flex to whatever the circumstances call for.

In this chapter, I will deal with some of the most common challenges around confrontation and give some foundational tips and techniques to help you confront a range of situations with more ease.

Confrontational situations come in many shapes and sizes. Some you can prepare for, such as handling tough questions at a meeting, any pushback from your boss when you ask for a pay increase, or handling a challenge with a loved one (you are used to how they'll behave) or preparing for serious objections during a meeting at work. Other confrontations may take you by surprise: an unexpected angry outburst from a colleague, a question or challenge you don't understand or have an immediate answer to, someone taking control of a conversation, or any other time when you are left wondering, 'Now what?'

Here's the good news. The skills for successfully handling confrontation situations that you are prepared for also apply to those that take you by surprise. It's true that the better prepared you are, the fewer surprises you'll get, and whatever you get, you'll handle with less stress. But let's face it, life is full of surprises you can't prepare for.

Preparation vs. Surprise

How can you be better prepared for confrontation? Certain situations require more preparation than others. Perhaps the stakes are high and you stand to gain or lose a lot depending on the outcome, so it's worth putting in the time to prepare your approach. For example, learn as much as you can beforehand about how the other person feels or where they stand on any issues, what other things outside your conversation may be affecting them, what do they stand to gain or lose? Like you, they will have an approach to confrontation and it would be helpful for you to be aware of it. Your knowledge will inform the way you confront them and increase the likelihood of a better outcome.

Once you know their approach to confrontation, you can benefit from adapting your approach so you can reduce tension and make confronting easier for yourself and the other person. For example, if you learn they are going to be tough, direct and interested in detail, do your homework accordingly and have well-prepared and supported answers and arguments. If you learn they are really uncomfortable with confrontation and may shy away from discussing difficult issues, you may decide to be patient, suggest alternatives or offer to be part of a solution in order to get a result.

As you can see, it is a two-way process and, when you can, knowing how the other person approaches or responds to confrontation is a helpful bit of insight.

Responses to confrontation

So, let's say you were taken by surprise by a particular confrontation. Maybe you weren't expecting someone to argue or push back with you or you got a negative response to your idea or proposal. It could be that you were asked a question that you had no clue how to answer or you felt embarrassed or affronted after a comment or statement made. Now what? Try this.

1. Maintain eye contact, relax your body, relax your jaw, keep your chest and shoulders open, with your weight balanced on both feet.

2. Take a calming breath and don't defend or get defensive.

3. Clarify what has upset the other person. Ask them if you need to – it is very likely that you won't know the answer, and asking goes a long way.

4. Once you understand, deal with it appropriately.

Let's have a look at some of the ways (scenarios) you can improve the ease and success of your surprise confrontation moments. Reflect on times when you faced situations where you weren't sure how to respond and make a plan to choose a few new behaviours for next time.

If you are surprised by a confrontation with someone whose approach appears aggressive, abrupt or direct:

- Keep your body upright and relaxed.

- Don't apologize, agree or make excuses.

- Be direct and well structured – if you disagree with them, tell them but ask them to explain their views further.

- Don't let them interrupt you. 'Let me finish, please.'

- Avoid sounding upset or angry.

- Maintain eye contact.

- Keep a strong tone in your voice without raising your volume above theirs.

- Conclude by restating what you have agreed.

If you are surprised by a confrontation with someone whose approach is focused on the detail:

- Stand or sit in a balanced posture and maintain eye contact.

- State what you see as the problem – don't offer a solution yet. Alternatively, let them start: ask them for a detailed explanation of what they believe the issue/problem is, and listen to their answer.

- Paraphrase back to them. If you disagree, say so and explain why.

- Avoid judgements and have your facts and examples ready. They usually remember most of the details of a conversation and will play it back to you later.

- Tell them that you would like to be able to come to them again should the problem continue.

 **If you are surprised by a confrontation with someone who appears uncomfortable or shy, or to be struggling with discussing the problem:**

- Choose a neutral place to have the discussion.
- Don't put the other person under pressure – keep it informal.
- Be careful to use facts and real examples – avoid judgements as you describe the issue/problem.
- Say how the problem makes you feel.
- Recommend a solution, or ask for their idea of a solution.
- Be prepared to be part of the solution – offer to help.

 If you are surprised by a confrontation with someone who appears sensitive to criticism, slightly disorganized or awkward in how they express their feelings:

- Acknowledge the positive aspects of their contribution.
- Paint the big picture – make sure they understand the importance of what they are doing and how they fit into the wider concept and objective.
- Be direct and positive, and use facts and examples.
- Avoid being judgemental.
- Ask them how they would like to solve the problem or make your own suggestions.

Confrontation default behaviours

Each of us has an unconscious preference for our behaviours while we are confronting or being confronted. Think about your own repertoire. For example, when you are seated or standing, where is your weight situated? Are your shoulders tense or relaxed? Is your jaw tight and your tongue firmly lodged in the roof of your mouth? What is your breathing like? Are you leaning forwards or back? The most common confrontation default behaviours involve an above average amount of tension in the body. These are some of them:

I do what I always do Sometimes we resort to behaviours that we have used in the past or that work with people we know. The challenge is they become our go-to response only because they have worked for us before. These responses are like a stopped watch – they are right twice a day.

'I do what I always do' can include bursting into tears, apologizing, pacing around the room, faking indignation, exaggeration, withholding eye contact or looking away a lot while you speak or listen, slouching your shoulders so that you appear 'defeated' or overwhelmed, crossing your arms and legs while speaking or listening, fidgeting, turning your face at an extreme angle while you speak or listen and appearing defensive, disbelieving or suspicious. When you are in these default postures, they inform your approach to confrontation. It is natural to want to reduce the tension by closing off from the other person and

expand the space between you by backing off or down, or looking away, and these behaviours may diffuse the situation in some cases. However, they may also be perpetuating a cycle/habit you want to change.

Your behaviours do not operate in isolation. Whatever you do will have an effect on the other person. These behaviours are not bad or good, but your ability to confront with more ease is affected by them. I had a friend whose typical confrontation default was to sit with her knees and body facing away from the listener, arms crossed with her head on a slant and eyes squinting, as if she was looking at the listener suspiciously. One day, during a friendly coffee break, I shared my observation. I asked her to make a subtle change by facing me fully without tilting her head. The change was remarkable. It felt so different – she was face forwards, relaxed, with full attention and not suspicious. She needed gentle reminders for a while after that not to ease back into her old posture but this small shift created an impression of greater ease about her, particularly at the start of any potential confrontation. The physical 'announcement' of how she was feeling before she even started, suspicious, defensive, uncomfortable, was replaced with alert, open, comfortable.

Playing nice This default behaviour is characterized by you becoming nicer, more accommodating, cleverer and funnier as you respond to a personal jibe or when you feel nervous or intimidated. But in doing so you are not actually confronting the issue at hand directly. This can often happen with people you care about or where you feel you could damage the relationship by standing up for yourself.

Physically, playing nice feels like you are pouring a bucket of cool water on a fire. Sometimes you can diffuse anger and danger by deferring. However, most of the time it will be a habit you want to change.

Let me give you some of the easiest ways to confront a personal jibe or habitual intimidation without playing nice:

- **Calmly ignore it** – 'Always put your oxygen mask on before helping others.' This is their problem and you don't need to feed it, now or ever. Stand tall, chin up, eyes ahead.

- **Calmly call it out** – if a behaviour is inappropriate or mean, simply say, 'I don't think that is appropriate', or 'Your taunting is disruptive and I'd like you to stop'.

- **Calmly clarify it** – this will allow you to stay constructively engaged with the other person and explore the situation more fully. Often your genuine efforts to explore are the most powerful and constructive way to play nice: 'Why do you feel that way?', 'What would you prefer?', 'Where did you get that information?' or 'Tell me more about how you came to that conclusion?' You'll often find the other person will back down or have no clear reason for their jibe and you'll learn you have no clear reason to feel intimidated or nervous.

When playing nice, it is important to be aware of using too much padding. You may take too long to get to your point, mention too many other things or 'sugar' the conversation so it becomes hard to recover and get back on track. In lessening the impact on you and the other person, you end up too far away from where you need to be.

Foundational behaviours

Creating personal strength, calm and clear-headedness during confrontation can seem challenging. The good news is that it is always possible. With practice and persistence you can feel and act more compassionately and objectively towards situations that in the past may have 'pushed your buttons' or caused you to overreact or walk away wounded or angry.

Match then balance This is a good place to start practising strength, calm and clear-headedness. When confronting or being confronted, be physically aware of listening and give full attention to another point of view. You can't really confront properly until you understand where the other person is coming from. As you do this, try to keep your bodies in equilibrium, meaning that if the other person is sitting, sit. If they are standing, stand. This balances the access to eye contact and matches energy levels. If you notice the other person is agitated, pacing or distracted, focus on being balanced on both feet, having a relaxed body while sitting or standing and maintaining eye contact while listening or speaking. Keep your jaw relaxed, fingers relaxed, toes and feet relaxed.

While standing, it sometimes helps to gently touch or position oneself against or lean on anchor on a conveniently placed piece of furniture. Refer to the 'neither here nor there' section (see page 51). Neither here nor there is a default movement posture where one stops

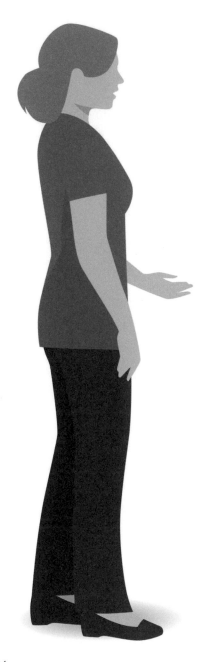

short of a meaningful distance from a place in the room. It equates to not finishing a movement and can create the feeling of lacking confidence or determination.

It may be necessary to take notes during your confrontation and it feels good to have something useful to do with your hands! (No, a device doesn't count unless you are using it to record.)

Make an effort to create the right environment for open, honest communication. Judge the content, not the messenger, and resist the urge to control the confrontation. Don't get defensive or take things personally.

Try to separate what you know first-hand from what may be second- or third-hand – this is the difference between 'knowing' and 'knowing about'.

When you confront well, it is because you have been concerned with respecting others and have been willing to negotiate and compromise where necessary. You keep your promises and are prepared to take risks. If you try something that doesn't work out, you don't take it too personally. When you avoid negativity and focus on the positive, you can motivate others and help them feel more positive about themselves.

Clarification is your true north
One of the cornerstones of effective confrontation lies in your ability to seek and gain clarity. Clarity often requires confrontation. It means that you may need to have the courage to stop the flow of a conversation at an inconvenient time, go back over something others think is obvious, ask a question at a critical juncture or when you think it might not be the right question or think you may have missed your chance or it is too late in the conversation to ask. Trust your instincts: if the issue is not clear to you, that's enough. It may not be clear to others, either.

Seeking clarification requires courage, relentlessness and as much objectivity as you can muster. Stand or sit with a balanced posture, face the other person (or group) directly and maintain eye contact, particularly after you have asked for clarification. Clarification also has a language and here are some phrases you could use:

'How do you think we should deal with...?'

'Tell me what you think about...'

'I feel...'

'What is your opinion?'

'Let's...'

'If I understand you correctly, you mean/this means/it means...'

'Let's see if I understand/ understand you...'

'Do you/Does this mean then that...?'

'So what you are really saying is...?'

'Would it be correct to say that...?'

'So, in other words...'

'Can I conclude from this that...?'

'What if...?'

'May I assume that...?'

'Am I right in assuming...?'

'Before we move on, I'd like to clarify something...'

Having a structure

The secret to being more comfortable with confronting people is having a reliable structure you can use, so that you know what you have to say and in what order. With a structure you can feel more confident and in control. You can confront anything if you understand there is a structure to it. Use the structure as your anchor and hang on tight in heavy weather.

So, how can structure help you confront with confidence? The order and structure of your message can, and will, affect the way the other person hears your information and responds to you. You are more likely to get a positive outcome if you have been sensitive to this. You can rely on structure to help you muster the courage to give it a try – if only because it will markedly increase your chances of success. Think of it as your lucky charm!

Tackle some of the little things first – you know what they are for you. Send back the insipid soup at the restaurant, tell your roommate to stop using household items without replacing them, ask for a change in your hotel room, and so on.

Here is a small selection of proven, everyday structures that I know work – I have used them for years with my clients. Confrontation may seem awful to you, but think of it as a bit like dancing. You never wanted to get out on the dance floor but you did and now there's no stopping you! It's the same with confrontation: stop taking it so seriously and try it.

Confronting someone you need You have some tough news to deliver to a person at work or in a professional setting, possibly your housekeeper, babysitter or caregiver.

Step 1: Be sure that you frame the problem as if you 'own' it yourself.

Step 2: Don't then state the problem. Instead, succinctly state the solution or action you want.

Step 3: Next, transfer the ownership of the problem.

Step 4: Make sure you repeat it and use the same language. It is common for the other person to introduce other issues or argue. Don't get sidetracked or involved with anything else, and don't justify your position.

Step 5: Listen for cooperation and play it back to them.

How this structure might work in practice:
Step 1: 'Molly, you are always coming in late' is accusatory and runs the risk of putting the other person on the defensive. Instead, start with words such as 'I'm concerned that...', or 'I'd like to talk to you about something that is bothering me'.

Step 2: 'I need you to be here at nine o'clock every morning'. Personalize it, making it 'I', not 'We'.

Step 3: 'How can you help me?' 'How can you solve this?'

Step 4: 'So you will catch the earlier bus or get a ride with your partner so you can be here by nine o'clock?'

Step 5: 'So what you are saying is you can be here by nine o'clock every morning', or 'Let me summarize what you have said'.

If you still get resistance, hang on in there. Don't let emotion creep in. Ask: 'What is blocking you from doing/achieving this?' Once you identify the blocker, stay objective and stick to how they may be able to find a solution.

Confronting someone you care about This one is good for spouses, teenagers, friends, family – for times when emotion gets in the way more easily, and there may be a history of approaching each other or arguing in a particular way. This may help you step out of the pattern.

Step 1: State the issue in one sentence.
Step 2: Give an example of the behaviour you want to change.
Step 3: Describe how you feel about it.
Step 4: Tell them what you think is at stake if the behaviour doesn't change.
Step 5: State how you may be contributing to the problem.
Step 6: State your desire to resolve the issue.
Step 7: Ask them to respond.

How this structure might work in practice:
Step 1: 'Wendy, I really want to talk to you about the effect your behaviour is having on some of our friends'.
Step 2: 'I found out that at our party last weekend you drank too much and were rude to Karen about how you think she is a pushy parent'.
Step 3: 'I am embarrassed, and concerned about the consequences'.

Step 4: 'If you can't control your drinking at our parties, I am worried that our friendships could be at stake.'

Step 5: 'I feel partly responsible because I could have stopped filling your glass so often or had a word with you earlier.'

Step 6: 'This is what I would like to resolve, Wendy. You're drinking too much and this inappropriate behaviour is a result.'

Step 7: 'I want to understand your perspective and what you think is going on. Please talk to me.'

Business is business This is all about returning something, complaining about bad service, a general 'I should have said something at the time' situation. Bear in mind that complaining when something is wrong is perfectly okay, indeed expected. Also, behave like a civilized person or you will get what you deserve. Customers have rights, but be fair. No one wants to help a mean person. Nine times out of ten the person you are complaining to is not the source of the problem. There is also a cultural context that will affect expectations on both sides.

Step 1: Be sure to find the right person to complain to.

Step 2: State upfront what you want the outcome to be. Do it politely, confidently and with full eye contact.

Step 3: If you don't get satisfaction immediately, keep your cool. Persist – this is where most people break down or give up.

How this structure might work in practice:

Step 1: Complaining to the wrong person is pointless. I have a mantra that goes: 'If you have heard ˝No˝, you have just spoken to the wrong person.' Start with: 'I would like to speak to the person responsible for...' – it is usually the manager or supervisor. Be firm, you want the right person.

Step 2: 'This is not what I was expecting, I would like my money back,' or 'I'm not satisfied with how this fits and would like to exchange it,' or 'I would like to talk to you about the bad customer service I received today and I would like an apology from the person concerned,' or 'My dress was stained by your server who spilled wine on it and I would like you to pay for it to be dry-cleaned.' A clear opening position from you and a statement of what you want will yield better results.

Step 3: Be firm, keep the same confident tone and maintain full eye contact. 'I'm not satisfied with your answer/solution.' Repeat what you want the outcome to be in the same cool tone. If you still don't get satisfaction, insist on speaking to a higher authority. If they are not there, get their name and make an appointment to see them or get a direct phone number. Don't leave without the details of the people you have been dealing with so far so that the next person knows the full story and the people you have dealt with and the dates. It is important to have the chronology. Save any receipts or paperwork. Continue to be cool-headed and fair: you want a solution and don't want to go away angry.

Saying 'no' Not being able to say 'No' is no laughing matter. It is a spiral that is difficult to get out of because it feels good to say 'Yes' and the people around you start to depend on it – and depend on it, and depend on it.

Step 1: Ask yourself if the request is reasonable – if there is any doubt, you probably don't want to do it.

Step 2: Most of the time, you need to get more information and clarification. Ask for it! Sometimes to get you to say 'Yes', people will leave out unsavoury bits of information. Understand exactly what they are asking for, and why they feel they need to.

Step 3: Resist the urge. If you don't want to do it at this point, say 'No'.

Step 4: Don't apologize. This is an important point. Don't say, 'I'm sorry but....' It's not your problem, so don't own it by apologizing for it. Also, if you do apologize, you give a signal to the other person that you are possibly open to persuasion.

Step 5: Instead, say 'No', clearly. Then pause briefly. Follow with your explanation of why you don't want to do it. If you want to or you care, help the person find another solution.

How to say 'no' in practice:
The key to saying 'No' effectively is to say it once and say it well. Stand firm, maintain eye contact and maintain silence afterwards. Below are some tips on ways to begin sentences or answer requests:

"No, thank you"

'I decided a long time ago never to...'

'No, thank you.'

'I would prefer not to.'

'No, thanks, that doesn't suit me right now.'

'No, I'm not interested.'

'No, I have other plans.'

'No, can I help you find an alternative?'

Compassionate interjecting Another important form of foundational confrontation is, what I like to call compassionate interjecting. It is compassionate because it shows respect and an interest in the greater good. Interjecting (as opposed to interrupting) is often needed in the spirit of moving things on when someone is monopolizing airtime, gossiping or needs a timely correction, clarification or refocusing.

If you are jumping in on a conversation or breaking up a monologue, be able to state your purpose succinctly. If you can, it is best to be as polite as possible and interject when the timing is easiest, say, when the other person has paused for a breath or there is a natural conceptual break in the flow of their monologue. Here are some sample behaviours and phrases that make this kind of confrontation easier.

'I have an idea that relates to what you just said.'

'Excuse me, I'd like to add something to that.'

'May I interject here?'

'I'd like to interject here.'

If you are trying to interject and it is not being acknowledged, use a gesture or some eye contact with the other person to let them know you want to say something. Even try clearing your throat. Sometimes it helps, where appropriate, to make a small step or gesture forwards at the same time. Say what you need to say and then let them get back to the conversation.

If you want to interject while a group is standing together talking, be sure to approach the group but don't 'join' the group or stand too close to the person talking. They may think you just want to stand and listen. Stand just far away enough to suggest you don't want to be part of the conversation, make eye contact with the individual speaking and then interject as needed.

It is always okay to interject for an explanation or to seek clarification. You'll often be surprised by how many people will tell you they were glad you did!

I find the following interjectables make good sentence starters for confrontation. This is when you need to jump in, speak up and/or be part of the flow of a conversation or meeting:

- 'May I stop you there for a moment?'
- 'I'd like to add something...'
- 'Could you explain that a little more?
- 'Let me paraphrase your question.'

- 'I agree...'
- 'As far as I am concerned...'
- 'That's correct.'
- 'I disagree...'
- 'I'm not convinced about that.'
- 'The way I see it...'

- 'It would be interesting to consider...'
- 'How about...?'
- 'Tell me more.'
- 'Say more about that.'
- 'What else should I know?'
- 'Describe...'

Being Confronted: a Look at the Other Side

The most unpleasant experiences associated with being confronted often come from being taken by surprise. Someone may disagree with you, verbally attack you, criticize you or just be plain nasty.

No matter what your confrontation style or experience, you can handle the confrontation. One of the hardest things to do when someone is confronting you is to remain calm and objective. It takes practice and courage. I would like you to think about it another way, too. As Miguel Ruiz says in his inspirational book, *The Four Agreements*, 'Don't take anything personally.' Taking things personally is actually the maximum expression of selfishness because we make the assumption that everything is about 'me'.

As I have said before, what others say about you (good or bad) or how they feel is their problem, not yours. Nothing they say or think is really about you. It follows then that you are not responsible for the actions of others, but just for your own actions. With this in mind, you can have the courage to be objective while being confronted.

You must then have the determination to understand the perspective of the person you are dealing with. If you know where they are coming from, you will improve your chances of defusing the tension and learning the real reason for the confrontation.

Dealing with criticism

Most of us find it hard to deal with the confrontation of criticism, even if it is fair. The rule here is if it isn't fair, don't take it personally. If it is fair, don't take it personally, but acknowledge it and consider it a gift.

Criticism isn't 'clean' or fair if it is laced with judgement. For example, 'You said you would call and cancel dinner with Joe and Sue and you haven't done it yet' is fair. 'You are trying to get out of it so I'll have to do it, won't I?' is judgemental. 'You're right, I haven't done it. I'll do it right after lunch today' is a positive response, acknowledging that the criticism is fair. Don't bite if the other person exaggerates or adds a judgement call. Take the high road, stay calm and in control of the situation.

If the criticism is personal in nature, seek first to understand. Ask a question to clarify, so you will either get a real answer and can deal with the problem or you will discover that the person is just being obnoxious and has no real problem at all. So, for example:

'Your friend Mark is always so patronizing to me and you never defend me – you are too busy having fun.'

'In what way do you feel patronized by him?'

Once you have established it is not just a case of paranoia or insecurity, or a way to pick a fight, you can explore the details of the problem and work towards resolving it: 'Does he always behave that way to you?' 'Why do you feel that I let you down – what is it you would like me to do or say, and do you think it would help?'

The important thing in this example is not taking the criticism at face value. Before responding by jumping to defend yourself (in other words, taking it personally), and thereby fuelling the confrontation, you need to work out why this criticism is being levelled at you and what is really behind it. Often someone is angry at something else but their ire is directed at you. Seeking to understand before you respond will be your protection against things getting worse. There are many ways of responding to an accusation or confrontation and finding the most appropriate response in each instance is essential if misunderstandings and grievances are to be resolved.

Responding appropriately in the moment

As this chapter has highlighted, the way you respond to someone who confronts you, whatever the reason, is important in contributing to how well things turn out. As witnessed in the example above, you have the intention to understand the context, but what if the other person is just being mischievous, mean or unfair?

Maybe they just want to unsettle you, or are jealous or showing off. If so, here are ways to deal with it:

- **Ignore it** – sometimes they may just be winding you up. Take away their power.

- **Use humour to defuse the tension** – be clear that you are not laughing at them but rather finding a funny side to the situation.

- **Walk away** – but be careful because it is hard to walk back in. Be sure you really want to do this. Subtly let them know you are aware of what they are doing – by holding eye contact, pausing, commenting on whether their behaviour is appropriate or necessary, even asking them to stop.

- **Stall for time** – give yourself space to think about your response. It could be minutes or hours or days. Often having some time to gather your thoughts before responding can help a lot. Don't be afraid to say that is what you need.

- **Ask a positive question** – you want to understand why they are saying or doing something. This doesn't mean sarcasm, so be careful of your tone. It is a genuine question, phrased in a positive way to get a clear answer. It may take them by surprise: 'Phil, I'm interested in how you feel. Why are you so angry?'

- **Give as good as you get but take the moral high road** – if someone does something underhanded or mean, you don't need to descend to that level. Rather, if someone is tough, be tough back.

Being successful at confrontation is partly to do with having the courage to try something new and partly to do with accepting confrontation as an invitation – so, just another part of life. Also, understanding what the other person is really talking about or where they are coming from means you can deal with the situation appropriately – and with more confidence and control.

The more comfortable you get with the idea of confronting, the less it seems to 'happen' to you. Start small and invest the time and effort and you will feel so much more at ease. For those of you who are comfortable confronting and may benefit from some refinement, jump in now! There are benefits to you, your relationships, wellbeing and career.

A confrontation manifesto

Let me give you some important principles to keep in mind in case you are ever in doubt in a confrontational situation:

- Don't take what's said personally. Whatever the other person thinks or feels, it is not your problem. It is their problem, because it is their way of looking at the world. They see the world through their eyes. It is up to you to decide whether you want to get involved in someone else's problems.

- You are entitled to your own opinions and feelings, and to express them to yourself and others.

- You are entitled to ask for what you want, although you should realize that the other person is entitled to refuse you.

- You are entitled to change your mind.

- You are entitled to privacy.

- You are entitled to achieve your goals and aspirations as long as you do not take unfair advantage of someone else.

- You will make the wrong decisions, sometimes. So what? Accept the mistakes, don't take them too personally and try again.

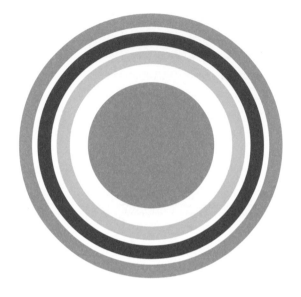

6

Cultivating Presence

Presence is a much sought-after quality. I'm glad that more and more people are exploring the idea of presence and what it means to them. The lovely thing about this exploration is that the journey will always start exactly where you are, and you are ready now. As the Spanish poet Antonio Machado said, 'Wanderer, there is no path. The path is made by walking.'

Presence is hard to define, yet most of us know it when we see it. A request I often get from clients is to help a team member who 'needs more presence' or to help people who feel they 'lack gravitas'. As I seek to clarify exactly what they mean by presence and what they think will be different if they 'have it', here are some common descriptors that pop up: 'I want to feel more confident and in control'; 'I want people to take me seriously'; 'I want to have command of the room', 'I want to be more calm and focused'; 'I want to be able to think on my feet', 'I want to stop being so self-conscious', 'I feel so physically awkward when the focus is on me' or 'I want to feel more connected to people'.

The insight that has emerged out of my countless coaching sessions, as well as studying years of research in the field of social psychology, is that presence is defined differently by different people. Presence is also partly determined by how you feel about yourself.

A combination of internal and external factors determines the calculus of presence. Internal factors include our own life experience and conditioning, our self-perception and sense of wellbeing. External factors vary depending on how others see us, the impressions we create and the context in which we find ourselves. In other words, presence is partly in the eye of the beholder.

Presence is when there is an 'alignment' between your inner world and your outer physical body. In other words, alignment is when what you are saying or communicating to others is consistent with your intention (feelings, beliefs, values, objectives in a given

'Wanderer, there is no path. The path is made by walking.' Antonio Machado

situation). More than that, alignment is observed and felt by others. By cultivating presence, you remove distraction and gently compel attention.

When you are aligned, you are more relaxed. When you are relaxed, you are more in the moment. When you are in the moment, you bring others into the moment with you.

Cultivating presence is an every-day-in-every-way goal that requires some learned skills in order to improve. It's not that we don't have moments of presence or have a calm confidence and a feeling of personal power in certain situations. We do. There are times, however, when we wish that, whatever presence is, it would be a more familiar state of being to us and to come when we call!

As I have discussed throughout this book, by increasing your awareness and implementing the foundational postures and responses, we are creating a more 'available' state of presence by allowing our body to support us. This support will offer us the psychological and physical edge to get us through our personal high-stakes situations at work and in our personal lives.

The good news is that you already have what you need to cultivate presence. This chapter will focus on the everyday skills required, and then explore some foundational postures and responses that will support you, in cultivating presence.

There are four elements to focus on that I believe will help you actively cultivate presence. All of them will support you in your efforts to be 'in the moment'.

I'll deal with each individually. None of them is any more important than the other. Rather, they support each other.

Quality of Listening

Listening is something you may spend your entire life not knowing that you are mediocre at doing. As a consequence, you will gain access to the benefits it can bring you and those around you. It is the skill that can move you forwards in life most quickly and in the most interesting ways.

Good-quality listening helps you discern the true nature of a situation, and understanding what is really happening in the moment makes you agile, flexible and capable of responding to your world in the most powerful way.

Studies show that most people think they are good listeners, because they have been told so by someone or because they don't interrupt others. Maybe you are the one everyone talks to or confides in. Perhaps you allow others to talk more than you do in conversation. But saying nothing does not make you a good listener.

The human body is hardwired to listen. The obvious way is through our ears and eyes. However, listening also happens through touch, smell, feeling, temperature, pulse, rhythm and gut feeling, or intuition – and most of us have only one or two channels tuned in most of the time.

A friend of mine once described listening as being 'a problem of attention'. He said that we often find it difficult to listen because our attention is tied or fixed to too many things. We are often thinking of what we did yesterday or have to do later today or tomorrow.

We encounter listening barriers every day. If we know about them, we can control them or reduce their impact. Default listening can be categorized into mental, emotional and physical barriers, and also our default listening postures.

Mental barriers: these include prejudice and judgement, and the knowledge you have about something (I'm the expert, why should I listen to these people?); how well or fast your brain processes the relevant information (gosh, I wish they would speak a little slower so I can write my notes clearly); planning (I didn't know so-and-so was going to be at this lunch – how does she fit in?); structure of the message (I didn't think there was a problem – why is she proposing a solution?); control (I wish she would stop talking, I want to tell my story); time (we are running over time, we will never get to dinner at this rate); observation (that person is sending strange signals – I don't know if I can trust him).

Emotional barriers: these include: fear (I can't go back and tell everyone I failed); lust (I wonder if he finds me as attractive as I find him); ego (I can't believe he thinks he knows more than me, I'll show him); greed (if I feign indignation, maybe I can get a better deal); self-consciousness (I wonder if they can tell I don't know a lot about this – I hope they can't see me blushing); doubt (do I deserve to be her? what if we can't agree?).

Physical barriers: these include: heat (this room is too hot, the sun is coming in through the window and boiling me); cold (I wish I had my scarf – it's freezing in here); physical discomfort (ugh, these trousers are too tight); arousal (I like the look of that); noise (oh no, the builders are next door – not now); hunger (when's lunch?).

Mental, physical and emotional barriers are always present. These are the things you think about or feel or do, instead of listening fully. Apply this to every single person you meet and you have a typical situation. Each person is listening only as well as they can. The world places barriers to listening in front of us most of the time. Start by being aware of what these barriers are for you, and then notice what might be causing them for others. Maybe it is because you jump to a quick judgement about someone even before they open their mouth. Maybe someone triggers a memory and you feel emotionally distracted. Maybe you are hungry, tired or uncomfortable. If you are willing to take notice, you can 'park' the barrier or remove it entirely, in order to listen more fully.

The good news is that most of the barriers relate to things you can control. If you can't – if you are unable to listen properly or alter the circumstances – you can at least decide to postpone the conversation. Sometimes a verbal response to a listening barrier can be as simple as saying, 'I would like to be able to focus on our conversation. It's really noisy here, let's move'.

Listening defaults

Let's now have a look at the most common listening defaults. These modes represent your 'quality' of listening. None of them is right or wrong. It is when we get stuck doing one of them most of the time or in an inappropriate context that we get into difficulties:

- Listening to be polite
- Listening to be right or confirm
- Listening selectively.

Listening to be polite This style of listening is when you are 'present but not accounted for'. You may be physically there – or on the other end of the phone – and may even look as if you are listening. You may nod, grunt, smile and show interest, but your intention is to be polite, not actually to engage enough energy to listen. You may remember very little except that a pleasant, if meaningless, exchange has taken place. Conversations at most cocktail parties, casual business meetings and chance encounters fall into this category as, unfortunately, do many of those you have with your partner and children when you're tired at the end of the day. This style is to do with survival or coping for the weary or uninterested. It is the style that is the easiest to get away with – the listening equivalent of taking a nap.

Of course, sometimes you have to listen to be polite, for survival's sake, and it can be the best option in some circumstances – such as when you are jet-lagged, don't really have anything to say, or just want to be there if

only in person, like the party you agreed to go to where you put in an appearance to show willingness, then go home as soon as possible. But listening to be polite can be habit-forming, which means you run the risk of missing out on something interesting or stimulating, or of not taking the opportunity to show someone you care by really engaging.

I have a friend who is regularly invited to openings of exhibitions and similar events. He really dislikes the social whirl, and describes predictable small talk as 'having the same effect as a sleeping pill' at the end of a long day. He has chosen to make the most of his hours of enforced polite listening, so he plays a game with himself to take his listening out of the realm of mere politeness, and to create interest for himself. His approach is to 'find something interesting in everyone' and ask a question that makes both parties think about the answer.

He has three key opening questions designed to elicit more personal, and therefore interesting, information early on in the conversation. The following are examples of his questions:

- 'What did you like most about the exhibition (or whatever subject)?', rather than 'How do you like the exhibition?'.

- 'If the organizers could have done one thing differently tonight, what do you think it should have been?', rather than 'Would you like another drink?'.

- 'How did you develop an interest in (your subject)?', rather than 'What do you do?'.

Next time you are in a potential 'listen to be polite' situation, notice your posture and how you are holding your weight. If you find yourself in a familiar listening position – weight fully on one hip, slouching into a chair, shallow breathing, maybe bouncing back and forth a little from toes to heels, or fidgeting – do something different. Make yourself a little uncomfortable by shifting to the other side or standing on both feet with equal weight, weight slightly forwards on your toes, shoulders relaxed and tummy tucked in. Stay there for a moment and see how it feels. If you are seated at a table, try to sit with the edge of the chair seat midway up your hamstrings, feet flat on the floor, spine relaxed but erect, shoulders relaxed. If you're not at a table, lean back in the chair but keep your weight on both buttock cheeks, shoulders relaxed, chin positioned as if you are trying to hold an orange gently between your chin and chest. Don't exaggerate this – just think about keeping your neck and shoulders relaxed and spine erect, without throwing your head back. And don't forget to breathe ....

Life is full of moments when we wish we were somewhere else. Often, though, these moments can provide us with a richness we never imagined – if we pay attention to them.

Listening to be right or to confirm Many of us have a habit of wanting to be right. For some it is a vocation – subject-matter experts of all kinds are paid to be right (the problem is that they bring it home with them). Some cultures and belief systems value the strong, outspoken leader, the confident, definite person, but these people can be so busy trying to be right or to leave a good impression that they don't hear what is actually going on.

People like this may well be right sometimes. This style is characterized by interruption, either by breaking in with a yup, yup, yup and finishing someone's sentence for them, or by waiting only long enough to let them stop before jumping in to talk about how you agree or have had an experience like that.

This style also 'interrupts' in the sense that the listener stops paying attention as soon as they have heard what they need in order to confirm what they were already thinking, and to start thinking about something else. It's almost as if they have 'ticked the box'. You can see it in their body language. Eye contact disappears or is sporadic, and they may even start doing something else. Their body is often leaning forwards as they speak or listen. The underlying motivation behind this listening behaviour is fear – fear of losing, fear of failing, fear of being wrong or of being seen to lack knowledge.

If you know such a person, asking them nicely to stop interrupting or to listen until you have finished may not be enough. 'John, let me finish, please' – if that doesn't work, perhaps try: 'John, it distracts me from my train of thought when you interrupt me or finish my sentences. Would you please wait until I finish?' While it won't necessarily deal with the underlying problem, it will help them to be more aware of how you feel.

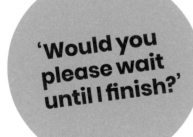
'Would you please wait until I finish?'

If you find yourself listening to be right or confirm, at the point you feel the need to say something while the other person is mid-sentence or mid-thought, resist the urge to interrupt. Just don't do it. Wait. Suspend your usual response – make a better choice. You'll get your chance to make your point, if it is still relevant, by the time the other person has finished. If they do get to finish, you will have created the impression that you are a generous listener and have done a good thing for them (they won't know of your internal struggle).

Another exercise is to practise active acknowledgement, validation and sharing while listening, but not adding your own commentary.

Acknowledgement refers to making small noises or gestures that coax or invite the other person to continue. Small grunts, hmms, ah-has, ohs, nodding slightly or very softly spoken words like 'really?' or 'I didn't realize that'. However, we've all met the annoying person who grunts or exclaims through our conversation to the point of distraction, and that's not what I mean.

The habit of listening to be right or confirm is a hard one to improve. However, if you chip away at the impulse to interject, you'll realize that you can often get what you need without having to be right or even having to be the one who makes the point.

One last thing: you can try some slow, steady breathing before you enter a discussion. Clarify the objective in your mind (if there is one) and have the courage to let your points pass. You may get more out of conversations than you're used to.

Listening posture defaults

Each of us adopts a few postures that we use most of the time, particularly while listening, and these vary wildly from person to person. The point is that they tend to appear and we then get stuck in them when we are in the above 'modes' of listening. The following are some of the most common. I am not saying that any of them are bad or good, but I believe that your ability to listen is affected by them.

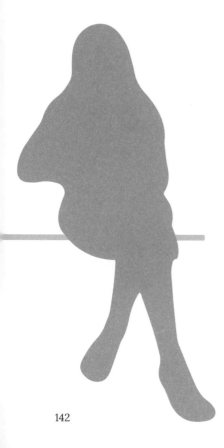

- Crossing your legs in a particular way while seated
- Keeping your arms folded while listening
- Shifting your weight onto one hip while standing or seated
- Turning your face at an angle to the person you are listening to
- Moving around, pacing the room
- Slouching your shoulders
- Looking away often while someone is talking
- Fidgeting
- Squinting your eyes or tilting your head.

Think about your own repertoire. When you are seated, listening to a friend or with a small group, where is your weight situated? Are your shoulders tense or relaxed? What is your breathing like? Do you tend to cross one leg over the other or slouch on one side? Do you lean into the chair to your right or left? The most common resting postures involve sitting low in the chair, legs crossed, head resting on the hand. How about when you are standing? Do you lean your weight on one hip and rest there? Is there a predominant handful of postures you adopt that you can identify? How are these postures affecting your ability to listen?

Foundational listening principles

Foundational listening is something that you won't aim to do exclusively, all the time. It takes some work and personal resilience to see it through. Think of it as aspirational, the check-and-balance to your unconscious habits. However, like all our foundational postures and responses, it is designed to create a more available state of presence when you need it. Below are the guiding elements. Do all of them and you are a saint. Do some of them most of the time and you are human – you've got the picture!

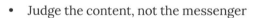

- Judge the content, not the messenger
- Resist the urge to control the conversation
- Own your accusations – keep it first person. 'I've heard such and such', not 'They told me'
- Don't get defensive or take things personally
- Find something you like about the other person (yes, there is always something – look for it early, keep looking)
- Listen to the person as if you had never met before

- Try to separate what you know first-hand from second- or third-hand – this is the difference between 'knowing' and 'knowing about'

- Don't interrupt. Listen on until the end, even if you know what the other person is going to say. Use follow-up questions – don't assume all has been said

- Allow about 20 per cent more time for listening than you think is necessary. Sometimes it takes longer than you expect to get to the good stuff

- Be sensitive – when people feel threatened, it is natural to get defensive. You may see aggression, anger, competitiveness. Forgive, understand, adjust what you are doing. Keep going. When your intention is to really learn about another person, you are non-judgemental and open on many levels. With a little practise, we are capable of listening on many levels at the same time. As with anything, you have to want to do it first.

You may know something or nothing about the person you are listening to, but you and they are willing to take the time and energy to discover a deeper understanding. This usually means you are listening with more empathy, may not be so quick to judge, and have a feeling for what is important for the other person as well as yourself. You are making the effort to listen more completely. This style of listening usually takes a little more time and attention to put into practice, but it's time well spent.

I have found over the years that the intention to listen in this way can actually cut the time it takes to get to the heart of any problem, because there is an interest in seeking the underlying reasons/motivations/feelings that may block success later on. It is also where the biggest gains come.

Some of the best listening experiences I have had have been with complete strangers. I know this sounds odd, but hear me out. Foundational listening requires that you listen to someone as if you don't know them. You listen generously, take time and are happy to go down unexpected pathways. You are curious. Your awareness is heightened. There is little or no judgement because there is no history and very little knowledge of your habitual responses. You are usually in a place where there may be the time to spare – a plane, a coffee shop, in a queue. It is the perfect place to practise this kind of listening. You may end up learning something about yourself, either by how you feel at the end of the conversation – refreshed, relaxed, energized – or because you see your own situation in a new way. You may even have gained a new insight into something.

Foundational listening postures

When you discover your particular default posture(s), you will notice that it feels comfortable to you. This is its charm but also its challenge. Often the most useful alternative, particularly for listening defaults, is to do the exact opposite or a variation of what you normally do. If you are sitting forwards, try sitting back; if you are leaning to one side, lean to the other. Make it definite rather than subtle. After a month or so, you are likely to find that you can listen to the world around you in a very different way. If you have ever practised meditation, you probably remember how challenging it was when you first started to sit silently for half an hour. Your body felt uncomfortable, or stiff, or twitchy. It wasn't until you practised waiting through this discomfort that you were able to reap the rewards of meditation. Well, it's a bit like that with listening.

This is an exciting challenge. Practise this with people you know, in both business and personal relationships. There is a bounty waiting to be mined, I promise.

As you become more aware, good-quality listening will continue to be a challenge. The essence of it lies in your intention to listen. It is not an easy journey, but it is an intensely rewarding one that takes practice every day. You can make big changes in subtle ways.

Paying Attention

Presence requires paying attention to yourself, other people and the task at hand. In my experience, the need to pay attention more fully is a problem that is common to many of my clients, and can be the key that unlocks the door to any change they want to make.

After learning how to pay attention fully, clients have told me that they get through the day using less energy and with lower stress levels. Some have said that they are more productive and the quality of their work is better; others that they get a sense of wellbeing, relief, calm and satisfaction. In many cases they have improved their ability to build rapport and relationships. So what do I mean by 'paying attention more fully' and why is it so important?

Think about the 100-metre sprint. As you watch the start, which of the runners do you think will win? The one who is tying his shoelaces, waving to his friends in the stadium and glancing sideways at his competitors, or the one who is focused, silent and looking in his lane towards the finishing line?

Paying full attention means that you are aware of being aware. You may also have heard this referred to as 'being in the moment' or 'being present'. Your body is generally relaxed and your breathing is slow. The opposite of this is being on 'automatic pilot' – the state in which most people spend their day-to-day lives and in which bad habits are allowed to repeat themselves.

Abraham Maslow, a noted American psychologist, described full attention as a 'peak experience', because at those times we 'joyfully find ourselves catapulted beyond the confines of the mundane or the ordinary'. But if it is so good, why aren't more of us doing it?

We all understand that our attention spans are challenged each day; our minds are full of chatter and our world is full of distractions. We're always being told that we are all busier than ever these days but sometimes I wonder, are we really? Do we have to be?

The distractions have weakened our ability to pay attention. As a result, we are less self-aware and have become less conscious of the impressions we create in others through our behaviour. Our world feeds this weakness with tailor-made, smaller-than-bite-sized chunks of information, gadgets designed to tune each other out as well as keeping us contactable 24/7.

Multitasking

Multitasking is a default attention response, but many people take pride in their perceived ability to do it. In most cases there is a false sense of achievement from performing many tasks simultaneously, but not doing anything well. Western work culture values hyperactivity but the rewards are few. Multitasking is an attention thief.

You have no doubt been on the receiving end of someone with whom you are conversing, whose attention shifts between you and their device or somewhere over your shoulder. The only thing they communicate to you as they multitask is that their attention is divided and not fully on you. You can't fake it.

Don't get me wrong, I don't think having many tasks on the go is a bad thing as such – it can often be necessary and productive. It works, for example, if you want to bake a cake and weed the garden in the same afternoon. So, you prepare the cake and put it in the oven, then go out and work in the garden. Multitasking meets your brain's need to do something new and exciting, while slowing your brain down and increasing errors. But you can't multitask your interaction with another person.

Paying attention to the wrong things

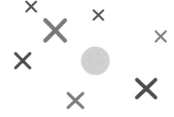

Another default attention response is paying attention to the wrong things. I find that when we are struggling with our attention, one of the first things to go is an ability to prioritize easily. The many tasks we need to complete become jumbled into a long to-do list where everything is equally important. A feeling of stress about being able to 'get it all done' takes over. Paying attention to the wrong things, not unlike multitasking, reveals itself to us in extremes.

For example, if you don't have a sense of priority, it looks physically like multitasking in that many things are happening at once with the same urgency or speed. Presence supports the alignment of your values and beliefs with your actions. If your priorities are not clear, your actions reflect that.

Paying attention to the wrong things can cause you to get bogged down in a task and not notice that the task is not progressing, just becoming more complex or constantly running into roadblocks.

Foundational attention

Let's have a look at some of the things you can do to practise paying attention more fully and reap the benefits. Attention is like a delicious piece of chocolate. It is better to savour each mouthful than to sit looking at the empty wrapper, asking yourself, 'Did I just eat all that?' Attention is finite and has a quality that runs from barely there to full and focused. You are, for the most part, in the driver's seat.

Many factors contribute to sharper attention. Getting enough sleep, the right kind of exercise, meditation, your general wellbeing and actively removing distractions.

The purpose of the following exercises is to help you sharpen your ability to pay attention to the present moment with awareness. I'd like to share a few exercises that I use to help clients. Speaking of chocolate ...

My dear friend is a health activist and Registered Nurse. She developed an exercise called Chocolate Mindfulness and did a TEDx presentation about it. I love this exercise (not only because, well, it's about chocolate) but because it is designed to remind us to practise slowing down and paying attention in the moment and to our senses.

The same principles apply to everything we have covered in this book. Paying attention to other people, their words, how you feel, what is happening around you. Savouring it.

Chocolate mindfulness exercise

Mindfulness is the invitation to slow down and pay attention to every detail of our current experience. A good place to practise this is to engage mindfully with our food. Take a full five minutes to do the exercise, taking only three mindfully small bites.

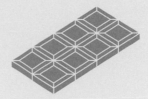

- Get yourself a 5 g (2 oz) piece of dark chocolate (or some other treat that you love).

- Begin with the sense of sight. Unwrap your chocolate and pause with it in your palm.

- Looking closely at the chocolate, notice its shape. Touch it, feel its smooth texture and notice its weight in your hand as you hold it. Take a gentle deep breath as you smell it. Engage the senses. Take your time. Enjoy the pleasure of anticipation.

- Now, lick the chocolate. Run your tongue over the chocolate and notice the intense flavours on your tongue. Look at it again. Smell it. As we do this, we trigger the chemical dopamine from our brain's pleasure centre. Our brain chemicals are engaging.

- Savour the chocolate by taking a small bite. Let it rest on your tongue as it begins to melt. Move the chocolate around your tongue, releasing the flavour. Savour the sensations and flavours.

- Before the next bite, look at the chocolate again. Take another small bite. Allow it to rest on your tongue, letting it melt. Nibble it and sensuously roll the chocolate around in your mouth, up to your palette, and be aware of every sensation.

- As you do this, your blood vessels are relaxing and your blood pressure lowering. The pleasure hormones associated with chocolate and mindfulness are also diminishing the inflammatory hormones that we all have present as a result of daily stress.

- As you finish the exercise, take another two minutes and enjoy savouring the moment – without touching your device!

Focused attention exercise

This exercise is designed to cultivate your brain's ability to focus on one object at a time, like your breath. Try starting at five minutes and build to 15 minutes if you can.

Sit in a comfortable, upright position and focus your attention on the sensation of breathing. Try to feel the sensation of coolness as you breathe in and out of your nostrils or feel your abdomen moving in and out. I have found that when you are starting out, focusing on something that is tied to your sensory experience, such as breathing and the movement of the abdomen, can be easier than focusing on counting or an external distraction, like a candle or a sound. Don't be disappointed if you have to retrieve your mind many times during the five-minute session. It's all good. Gently redirect it as it jumps away.

You can also do a focused attention exercise while walking. I love this because it combines a moving 'break' with the benefits of practising attention. This can be done indoors or outdoors. Try it with your feet on the ground, the air caressing your skin, the sunlight gently touching your face, the sounds in the air. I also like to focus on the feeling in my feet as I walk barefoot across sand, wood, grass or any friendly surface you like.

Open monitoring exercise

This exercise is about remaining open to any experience that arises – internal or external – and letting any barriers to listening or attention wash over you. The key is to not process it or not think about them as they arise, but to let them pass by you. Notice what comes to mind and let it pass.

Sit in a comfortable, upright position. Notice any sensations, thoughts or emotions that arise without holding onto them. Let go of any 'worrying', 'planning', 'judging', 'remembering', naming them as they appear. Then let them pass like clouds in the sky. You are just watching thoughts pass through your mind, rather than resting on them and letting them linger. If you find yourself getting stuck on anything, go back to your focused attention exercise to steady yourself.

Attention is a complex process and fundamental to cultivating presence. It includes feeling alert and aroused, deciding what we attend to or not, and staying focused when we need to. Attention needs exercise and practice to fine-tune it.

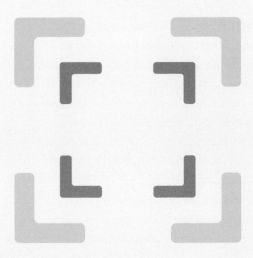

Managing Responses

Presence requires that you manage your responses. Doing so involves being thoughtful and consistent, and aligning your values and beliefs with your behaviour. Also, your efforts to cultivate presence can be disrupted in an instant by habitual responses. In a world that rewards 'action' and 'doing', giving a considered or appropriate response is not something we do naturally or easily. As a consequence, getting it right does not come naturally. I will focus on three of the most common default response behaviours:

- Keeping your mouth shut
- 'It's my way or the highway'
- Choosing your battles.

Keeping your mouth shut

Most of us throw our common sense out of the window when we are faced with an emotionally charged situation. We all have different ways of dealing with emotion and when the tension rises, some of us get ultra cool and silent, while others become louder and more boisterous. Either response is appropriate – *when* it is appropriate.

Herein lies the problem. I have had a number of clients over the years who limited their career options because of the way they mismanaged responses. The most common type of problem I was asked to deal with in the workplace was how people react to their emotional tension. Some people have a habit of lashing out in anger at a friend, embarrassing someone in a meeting by arguing with them or putting them down in front of others. It isn't serious enough to lose a friend or get fired, just enough to keep them from being promoted or becoming a productive member of their team.

This also happens in our personal lives. Certain people just know exactly how to upset us. Sometimes it is very difficult to know how to avoid the same old thing. They press the button, you respond! Sound familiar?

I know, you can hear your conscience saying, 'I told you so – you never listen to me.' But there are a few common-sense guidelines to consider before responding to an emotionally charged situation or provocation:

✓ It is important to think about the consequences of an argument or the action. Is it worth it?

✓ Don't get involved in something that's none of your business.

✓ If you are angry, identify what is behind your anger before you rush in and address the wrong issue.

✓ Make sure that what you say or do is going to solve something.

✓ Don't say something just because you 'feel you've been challenged' or get involved 'because you have been asked'.

✓ Ask yourself, 'Is it really a big deal?' Chances are that it's not.

✓ Realize that it often it takes a better person to simply let a conflict go.

✓ Ask yourself, 'Is there really a "right or wrong" for this issue?'

✓ Is this an issue you'll remember in the future? If not, don't take it on.

There's a technique called HALT, which means being prepared not to say or do anything for a moment if you're Hungry, Angry, Lonely (or hurt), Tired (or under time pressure). If you are any of these, halt. Eat the meal you skipped, calm down if you're angry, don't hide away if you're lonely or hurt, take a break if you are overworked. Obviously, if you're in two or more of these states, you really need to halt! HALT is a useful tool because so often immediate, physical or knee-jerk responses result in us saying or doing something we wish we hadn't.

It may mean keeping out of an escalating conflict; holding your tongue instead of saying something you may regret; not answering an emotionally loaded question on the spot; waiting to make an important decision; not saying or doing anything until you take time to figure out your feelings. Practise saying, 'I'll get back to you on that,' or 'Let me think about it first.' If you are being prodded to drop what you are doing, you could say, 'I'm progressing pretty well right now and I'm not sure how much longer I will be. I will let you know as I get closer to my finish time.'

The key is to be consistent and stick to what you have said you will do. In other words, don't move the goalposts or create a situation where you might have to. Don't exaggerate or fudge the response. Keep it neutral. When unthinking comments are not one-offs but a continual stream, they can erode credibility and damage relationships.

I'm not suggesting you don't show empathy when reacting emotionally, just that you need to be in a better position to choose a more considered response.

It's my way or the highway

Always needing to be right and in control has got to
be one of the most tedious personality traits on the
planet. This kind of behaviour chips away at the ability
to cultivate presence mostly because it is hard-focused
on a future outcome, rather than the insights of the
present moment.

My apologies to those of you who throughout
your life have put time and effort into perfecting
the art of control – I don't mean to upset you. Well,
maybe I do, actually.

'It's my way or the highway' means refusing to yield
or compromise. It is important to know when not to
hold your ground, be stubborn, be right or obstinate,
because it puts you and others into a 'corner'. This
attitude is a major obstacle to listening and to
developing relationships with others.

One of the most common types of challenge I am
asked to become involved with is the person who
believes that they know best and are always right, and
they are not always very nice about it. This is a problem
not only because of the difficulties it creates when
working in a team, but also because the truth is that no
one person has all the answers. Unique as each one of
us is, there is always someone out there who could do
our job as well or better.

Choosing your battles

Choosing your battles means not letting other
people erode your efforts to cultivate presence.
When it comes to making decisions about getting

into relationships – business or personal – we are all human: we make mistakes when 'reading' others and feel as if 'we should have seen it coming'.

The first principle is that you don't deserve to have bad or troublesome people in your life. Really! This means you need to set personal boundaries that allow you to take care of yourself. You effectively draw a line in the sand, past which you will not walk. It means you are not prepared to accept certain kinds of behaviour.

The second is that you must be prepared not to blame others for the way you feel, or to judge them. 'You hurt me, you embarrassed me, you deceived me', and because of that 'you are weird or mean or stupid'. It's not about them, it's about their effect on you, and you need to concentrate on this being your priority.

By not blaming or judging, you can be more objective and stay free of value judgements, something that may involve you unnecessarily. Instead, try standing back and thinking, 'That person seems fearful or full of anger and it would be better if I was not involved with them.' If you think about it, all you can really do is observe them. The rest is guesswork.

There are sometimes other, darker forces at work that guide us into repeating bad habits, but we won't be able to deal with them here – save them for your analyst! But aside from these, and even without the benefit of perfect foresight, setting boundaries can help you retain some control when embarking on new relationships and so provides an easier escape hatch should you decide you want out.

You have to set the boundaries in the knowledge that other people may not be willing or able to change their behaviour – and be prepared to take whatever action you need to if that proves to be the case. That action may be as dramatic as cutting someone out of your life completely. Sometimes we are afraid to set boundaries because it means hurting someone, making others angry or losing a relationship. But remember that it's worth standing up for yourself, even if people don't like it or may go away.

Setting boundaries is good for you and those around you. Here are some suggested responses if you feel you need to stand up for yourself.

- 'I need to communicate if we have a misunderstanding.'
- 'I won't accept your condescending jokes or your criticism.'
- 'I won't be disrespected – if you won't respect me, stay away.'
- 'If we are going to work together, I need honesty, respect and fairness.'
- 'Don't vent your anger on me – I won't have it.'
- 'I want openness in a relationship – your withholding is making our relationship unsatisfying for me.'

There is an unsavoury irony to all this. People who attract problem people are usually those who have a desire to be liked and/or a generous and trusting nature. You can't deal with the forces that may drive this behaviour, but believe me when I say that by replacing the behaviour, you can go a long way towards making it less of a problem.

Lie detection tips

It's helpful to know how people can betray themselves when they are not telling the truth.

- Higher-pitched voice than expected, hesitation, using the wrong words, bad sentence structure, unusual eye contact, dilated pupils, blinking or frequently rubbing the eyes.
- Inappropriate laughter – too much or too loud.
- Their bodies may be rigid. Because they are trying to overcontrol their body, you may see conflicting signals such as shrugs and grimaces, fidgeting hands and feet, a smiling mouth but unsmiling eyes, oversized gestures compared to what they are saying, or very small movements drawn into the body.
- Inappropriate sighing or shallow breathing.
- They might put physical barriers between you – a briefcase or handbag, a table, folded arms, books or papers.
- They may overcompensate by looking too relaxed, nonchalant, going into too much detail, using too much eye contact.
- They may ramble on about things that are irrelevant or inconsequential.
- They may become defensive or use humour or sarcasm in an attempt to avoid a subject.
- They may repeat back your exact words to answer a question, such as answering 'Did you take my socks?' with 'No, I did not take your socks.'
- When asked to describe a situation where they were unsuccessful, they will not usually talk about the negative aspects, the things that went wrong. They may also blame others.

The importance of wisdom

There was some research conducted recently to determine what it is that makes a person wise. Believe it or not, there are people called 'wisdom researchers', who have been studying the subject for years. One of them, Stephen Hall, explained some of the qualities of wisdom, which included 'a clear-eyed view of human nature, emotional resiliency and the ability to cope in the face of adversity, an openness to possibilities, forgiveness, humility, a knack for learning from lifetime experiences ... Emotion is central to wisdom, yet detachment is essential.' He added, 'Action is important, but so is judicious inaction.' In other words, knowing when not to act. The research also stated that while wisdom is generally found in those with more life experience, it is not limited to older people. Often wisdom can come from adversity or even experiences from early childhood that have shaped your outlook on life.

Researchers have devoted many years to developing metrics for measuring wisdom, and one thing is certain: people who score low on the wisdom scale tend to have a 'preoccupation with self'. I believe, though, that this is due to a lack of practice. I think one can practise wise behaviours and, in doing so, become wiser. Don't be fooled, practising wise behaviour is not easy. How often have you felt that inappropriate words 'just came out of my mouth' or confessed afterwards that 'I didn't realize what I was doing'? This is common, owing to a general lack of awareness about how we affect others. This is what the wisdom researchers I mentioned earlier refer to as 'preoccupation with self'.

So practising wise behaviours has a double benefit. It will help you understand how your behaviour affects others (thus be wiser) and to make better, more informed responses (thus be wiser).

Knowing when not to act is not, after all, very mysterious. Unless you find yourself in a cycle of repeating things you regret – which is a different matter – you can go quite a long way simply by knowing how to extricate yourself from the inevitable slip-up. Success at this is partly to do with having the courage to try something new, and partly to do with already having had the experience to know better. Still, we make mistakes. I think on the road to wisdom you can behave wisely.

The power of the apology

Many people get themselves into difficult situations because they can't acknowledge they are wrong. They are not comfortable with apologizing, and this inability or reluctance to say sorry leaves them with a lot of regret or damaged relationships.

The wonderful part of an apology is its power. It can mend a broken heart, soothe wounded pride or heal a fractured relationship. Particularly if you are in the wrong, or if you just want to start somewhere, there are some important steps to take. According to psychologists, there are three aspects to a successful apology. These are: being willing to accept

sorry

responsibility for your actions ('Mum, I was out of line and I am sorry'), regretting what you did ('I feel terrible about it') and being willing to take some action to remedy it ('I'll never do that again. I will apologize directly to everyone for my behaviour').

Let's say that you are in a situation where you and another person are both to blame. You may have had a heated argument at work about a matter that the next day seems trivial. One of you needs to initiate an apology. Doing so sets the scene for the other person to apologize, too. The next day at the coffee machine you say, 'I think we owe each other an apology. I'd like to start by saying I'm sorry for yesterday's misunderstanding.' The only catch is that you have to be ready to do it without any resentment or caveats.

It is possible that the other person doesn't agree, is still upset and is unwilling to accept your apology. That's okay – you have done your bit and you need to accept that they may not come around to your point of view. You can at least feel better because you have admitted the mistake and are showing you empathize with how your actions may have affected someone else. And however complex or long-running an argument or problem might be, a genuine apology, as a gesture of goodwill, is a good start.

Apologies are a little like going swimming in cold water. If you do it a little at a time, it can be painful. You have to go in full body, and once you are in, the water's fine! There are times when you should not apologize – that is, when you don't feel you are in the wrong. Be sure you are responsible for something before you own it.

Being Comfortable with Silence

Are you uncomfortable with even brief moments of silence? Do you feel the need to look at your device, listen to another podcast or have background noise for the sake of it? I know several people who can't sleep without their television or noise machine on. Do you feel compelled to do something rather than just sit silently for a few moments?

Getting/being comfortable with silence is key to cultivating presence. Silence is addictive. Once you get a taste for it and what it can do for you, you'll be hooked. It is where you source the strength to do what you need to do. Think about silence as space between thoughts. For most of us there is no such thing. The truth is that we need silence, both personally and professionally. We need to make the moments of space available to ourselves.

Default behaviours around silence

The following are behaviours we tend to adopt when we're uncomfortable with silence. The first two are the most common:

- Talking too much
- Creating a distraction through movement
- Jumping in with advice before an issue is clarified
- Using a break or silence in conversation to create a distraction and change the subject

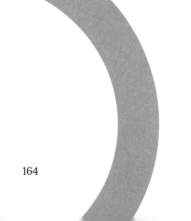

- Interrupting by talking over someone else

- Thinking about your response before someone has finished talking

- Responding quickly with little or no thought

- Attempting to be clever, charming, competent, impressive and talking in circles with nothing new emerging.

We are not taught to like silence. Many of us struggle with how to manage silence in negotiations, conversations, presentations and meetings. There is a general fear of a silent room – 'What if nobody says anything?' or 'The silence seems to go on forever', even when it is really just seconds. We believe that our answers have to be quick and ready; we need explanations and to demonstrate action, movement and confidence. The result is that we talk at each other, not with each other. We are so busy being an 'expert' or dynamic and clever that we fill up the airspace as if we are in transmit mode. As a result, we often miss what may really be going on.

Talking too much

Most people who talk too much have been told this overtly or otherwise by friends and family. People who do talk a lot believe that it is a positive trait and equals dynamism or high energy. Usually, though, talking too much stems from a discomfort with silence during conversation rather than being because one has a lot to say.

Practising not talking is a simple and relevant remedy for people who talk too much, but often there is a need to practise silence in other parts of their life as well as in speech. It's not as simple as asking someone to 'just stop talking'.

I have a family member who is considered 'talkative'. She has a ready story, example or comment for most discussions and has a tendency to 'think out loud' which makes her 'airtime' even longer. She interrupts other people's stories by adding her own. As a result people avoid her at gatherings.

I asked her to pause quietly for one or two breaths before responding. This sounds a little mechanical but it gave her a useful and challenging guideline. She told me that after two weeks of practising this breathing technique, she found the quality of her conversations took on a new dimension. With this short pause, she noticed how others jumped in to fill the silence, said something else or clarified, giving her interesting insight. Other people spent more time talking and there was a more balanced sharing of the airwaves.

These few techniques were difficult for her at first, but after three weeks, she had a respectable groundswell of people commenting that she seemed 'much more relaxed' and 'engaged'.

Making space for silence can mean not talking or avoiding noise. However, the kind of silence I want you to pursue is in moments between thoughts – where you do not actively distract yourself from silence.

Distracting through movement

We also show our discomfort with silence through extraneous or distracting movement, which in most people creates unnecessary tension and fatigue in the body. It can also affect posture and general alignment.

Most people who use movement, or 'busyness', to mask a discomfort with silence tend to share certain characteristics:

- Shifting, rocking or leaning into one or the other hip; they rarely have their weight on both feet at any one time

- Walking at uneven speeds – even short distances will combine a quick burst with stops and some meandering steps

- Bumping into furniture or doorways more often than the average person

- Fidgeting, twitching, tapping their foot, having something in their hand (lots of twisted paper clips and sweet wrappers); they also fiddle with buttons or threads on clothing

- Standing too close or too far away in social situations

- Never appearing to 'finish' the movement – tasks may get unfinished or items put back in the wrong place.

My colleague Anna is a good example of distraction through movement or busyness. When she stood still, she was moving. When she sat down, she was moving. But her movement didn't always have a purpose or function. It was usually subtle and not always immediately perceptible. Standing still, she shifted her weight slightly from foot to foot. Sitting, she would often change her weight or position, or tap her foot. There was always something in her hands – a pen, some notes, a wrapper that she was twisting.

I did some exercises with her to see how she felt when she didn't move as much or wasn't so 'busy'. Her discomfort was palpable, particularly if she had nothing in her hand or if she wasn't fidgeting or tapping her foot, or if she sat still for too long (meaning for about one minute). She referred to it as 'nothing happening'.

But not moving was the path to Anna's 'silence'. She needed to understand that 'nothing happening' gave listeners a chance to absorb what she was saying, for insight to occur, for her to emphasize what was important and to demonstrate her power and strength.

Meditation and comfort with silence

There are many traditions and countless ways to practise meditation and everyone needs to find what is right for them. There is no religious foundation required. The key to success is patience with yourself.

You can incorporate breathing, walking or writing into ways of beginning to practise silence. We can all benefit from more silence in our lives. Start in small ways to get a taste for it. Rather than going from morning to night without a break from distraction, steal a few moments in your everyday activity for silence.

If, now and then, you can go alone to a café, just sit quietly and eat your meal or drink your coffee without a newspaper or book. See what happens. Don't be

Relaxing meditation

This is my favourite meditation for relaxing and settling the mind.

- Select a suitable place for your meditation, ideally a quiet, peaceful spot, although I often meditate on planes, trains and wherever I can find spare moments to reconnect or re-energize.

- Sit in a comfortable position, resting your hands in your lap, with your eyes gently closed. Stretch your shoulders and neck to release any residual tension. When you are ready, take three deep, cleansing breaths. Release all the worries and tensions of the day. Let go of thoughts or plans. It is normal and okay for your mind to wander. Gently lead your mind back to your breath. Do this for two minutes.

- Next, relax into your natural breathing, allowing it to settle into its own pace, not too fast or too slow. Bring your attention into this moment by focusing on the gentle, rhythmic movement of your breath. Gently in, gently out. Let go of any thoughts about the past or the future and settle into the present moment. Allow your mind to rest in the simple rhythm of your breathing for five to 20 minutes.

- Establish a regular time to meditate if it suits your schedule or temperament (I don't meditate at the same time every day or even in the same place). Choose an app if you prefer to be guided – there are some wonderful choices. Daily meditation will eventually be like bathing or brushing your teeth. It can become a regular cleansing of your heart and mind.

Body scan exercise

This is my favourite exercise before bedtime or during a long flight. It can take three minutes or 30 minutes. I like it as a guided exercise with audio, but it is also effective if you do it with your own inner voice. One of my favourite audio versions, which lasts three minutes, is from UCLA in California. Improving the quality of your attention and your comfort with the silence that goes with this scan is a benefit that you will begin to enjoy immediately. Keep at it and don't despair as your attention ebbs and flows and behaves like an elusive creature! It will improve over time.

- The body scan is essentially like taking a flashlight and directing it systematically through your entire body. Start by focusing your attention on your toes, taking note of whatever sensations you feel. Relax your toes and your feet. Do you feel any tightness, tingling, cold, warmth?

- Next, move to the soles of your feet, your arches, your heels, ankles, knees, thighs, stomach and so on, slowly and deliberately moving the flashlight up your body. Take time to linger in an area if you feel you need to, noticing any sensations.

- Leave yourself time to gently finish the exercise by resting for one or two minutes afterwards.

self-conscious about being alone. Someone once said to me that they felt silly sitting alone in a restaurant. The truth is that you think about yourself more than others think about you. Even the busiest places offer us an opportunity to practise silence. Remember, I want you to pursue moments between thoughts where you do not actively distract yourself from silence.

Another technique for becoming more comfortable with silence is, as you go about your everyday activity, stop when you can and ask yourself, 'What part of me is resting?' By doing this, like my friend at the red traffic light, (oops, from an earlier iteration), you can start to observe your unique physical state and create a conscious moment of rest or silence. Be assured, there is always a part of you that is resting.

It is my hope that you will develop comfort with silence by practising it and using the suggestions in this book. If you think about it, silence is where you really can get something from nothing! Remember that silence is not just the absence of noise, but being still or at rest.

Cultivating presence is something that you do step by step and every day. When you are consciously cultivating, you will actively choose actions that support your growth. Focus on the quality of your listening and attention, how you manage your responses to yourself and others and seek opportunities to practise your ability to get comfortable with silence.

These elements will improve the richness of your experiences and those around you, and be your clearest path to personal presence.

Index

Acknowledgements

Author acknowledgements

My heartfelt thanks to Victoria Marshallsay and the team at Eddison Books in London, UK for their savvy, vision and enthusiasm. I am inspired every day by the women I work with; my clients, friends and family. I am blessed with a circle of brave, smart, wise women who are a vibrant source of insight, ideas and guidance.

Remember the words of Glinda the Good Witch from the movie, *The Wizard of Oz* 'You Had the Power All Along, My Dear'.

Picture credits

Illustrations by Paul Oakley except the following: ShutterstockPhotoInc. pages 47, 50 arrows; pages 87, 162 Sentavio; pages 90–91 Terpsychore; page 142 Nadzeya Shanchuk; page 147 Evgenii Matrosov

Chocolate Mindfulness Exercise, page 151: Robin Mallery, Tedx Evansville 2015

Eddison Books Limited

Managing Director Lisa Dyer
Senior Commissioning Editor Victoria Marshallsay
Copy Editor Helen Ridge
Proofreader Jane Donovan
Indexer Christine Shuttleworth
Designer James Pople
Production Gary Hayes